THE SUFFRAGETTE TIMELINE

An introduction to the Suffragette's epic struggle to win Votes For Women

By
Suzanne Keyte

Copyright 2018 Suzanne Keyte

All rights reserved

No part of this book may be reproduced in any form without the prior permission in writing of the author, except for brief quotations used for promotions or reviews

For more about all things Suffragette, please visit my pages at:
Facebook.com/SuffragetteLife
www.SuffragetteLife.co.uk

Published by
Golden Manor Press

The Suffragette Timeline

To all the courageous women who suffered so much to win a right we all now take for granted

And...
To all the women who value this brave struggle;
Please use your vote every chance you can!

TABLE OF CONTENTS

INTRODUCTION

LEADING FIGURES

GLOSSARY OF SUFFRAGE SOCIETIES

PART ONE – THE SUFFRAGETTE TIMELINE
19th Century
1900-1905
1906-1907
1908
1909
1910
1911
1912
1913
1914
1915-1917
1918-1928

PART TWO – SUFFRAGETTE STORIES
1. Adela Pankhurst
2. Suffragette postcards
3. Suffragette games
4. The 'Cat & Mouse Act'
5. Suffragists versus Suffragettes
6. Suffragette colours and medals
7. May Billinghurst
8. Frederick Pethick-Lawrence
9. The Suffragette Garden
10. Vera 'Jack' Holme
11. Nancy Astor MP
12. 'Black Friday'
13. Mary Jane Clarke
14. The Suffragette with the whip

SOURCES

INTRODUCTION

February 2018 marks the 100th anniversary of women being granted the right to vote in Parliamentary elections in Great Britain for the very first time

With the First World War still raging, on 6 February 1918, the British Government finally passed the 'Representation of the People Act', which allowed all men over twenty-one and women over thirty (with a property qualification) to vote. While all men could now vote for the first time, millions of younger, working class women were still denied that right. However, it was a massive step forward in the women's suffrage campaign and allowed 8.5 million women to vote in the Parliamentary elections in December 1918. The total electorate increased from eight to twenty-one million, but a huge inequality still remained between women and men.

One of the most significant reasons for the passing of the Act in 1918 was the need to allow the men returning from the battlefield to vote for the first time. The Government feared profound social unrest if the men of Britain, who had been fighting for King and Country for four long years, were still deemed not worthy to vote. It was also feared that if women were to achieve the vote on the same basis as men, they would outnumber them at the voting booths: a step the nervous Establishment was not prepared to take. In fact, many women in their twenties, who had contributed hugely to the war effort in dangerous jobs like munitions factories, were still denied a vote.

Suffragists and Suffragettes both held celebratory meetings in 1918, although these were somewhat muted as the war was still ongoing, and there was a recognition that this Act hadn't gone far enough.

It would be another ten years with the passing of the 'Equal Franchise Act of 1928', sadly just three weeks after the death of Emmeline Pankhurst, that women finally achieved the same voting rights as men.

The campaign for women's suffrage lasted six decades. From a few progressives in parliament arguing to widen the franchise, to hundreds of thousands of women demonstrating on the streets, it is a story which has many fascinating elements.

Despite sharing the same ultimate aim, some bitter divisions existed within the women's movement. The Suffragists (led by Millicent Fawcett), who believed in a campaign of constitutional argument in Parliament, became increasingly appalled by the militant tactics of the Suffragettes (led by Emmeline Pankhurst), who argued that only direct action, 'Deed Not Words', could win votes for women from an Establishment desperate to cling to power. From 1907-1914, the campaign turned ugly with numerous acts of vandalism and arson by the Suffragettes, and a brutal repression by the (supposedly) Liberal government.

Even with the shortcomings of the 1918 Act, its significance should still be celebrated. This was a massive victory on the long journey towards universal women's suffrage and was the culmination of decades of campaigning and demonstrating, and for some brave women, years of hardship, imprisonment and forcible feeding.

Told via more than 250 historical events, this is the amazing year-by-year story of the campaign to secure for women the basic human right to vote which we now all take for granted.

LEADING FIGURES

Emmeline Pankhurst – leader of the WSPU and most famous Suffragette

Christabel Pankhurst – exiled to Paris and architect of the rise in militancy

Sylvia Pankhurst – socialist who campaigned in the East End of London

Millicent Fawcett – long-standing Suffragist who rejected militancy and violence

Annie Kenney – working class activist, who (with Christabel) was the first to go to prison

Flora Drummond – leading organiser of rallies, marches and demonstrations

Emmeline Pethick-Lawrence – organisational power behind the WSPU

Emily Wilding Davison – most famous Suffragette martyr who died after direct action at Epsom

Mary Jane Clarke – Emmeline Pankhurst's sister and the first Suffragette to die for the cause

Lady Constance Lytton – aristocratic Suffragette who was force fed under an alias

Ethel Smyth – vigorous campaigner and composer of 'March Of The Women'

GLOSSARY OF SUFFRAGE SOCIETIES

National Society for Women's Suffrage (NSWS) – first national society to campaign for women's votes was formed in 1867 by Lydia Becker

Women's Liberal Federation (WLF) – formed in 1886 as an umbrella organisation for local Liberal Associations, by 1904 it had 67,000 members across almost 500 affiliated bodies

Women's Franchise League (WFL) - short-lived society formed in 1889 by Emmeline and Richard Pankhurst

National Union Of Women's Suffrage Societies (NUWSS) – various regional suffrage societies merged in 1896/97 to form a national organisation led by Millicent Fawcett. The leading moderate, constitutional campaign group

Women's Social And Political Union (WSPU) – founded in 1903 by Emmeline and Christabel Pankhurst, and became the leading militant Suffragette organisation, under the slogan 'Deeds Not Words.'

Women's Freedom League (WFL) – Led by Charlotte Despard, split from WSPU in 1907, over concerns about rising militancy

Artists Suffrage League (ASL) – formed in 1907 to design and create propaganda materials for the women's suffrage cause, most often the NUWSS

Women's Tax Resistance League (WTRL) – formed in 1909 as a direct action group (associated with the WFL) that used tax resistance to protest against the disenfranchisement of women

Suffrage Atelier – founded in February 1909 as a group of artists to raise money and support for the WSPU and WFL

Anti-Suffrage Organisations
Women's Anti-Suffrage League and Men's League For Opposing Women's Suffrage, both formed in 1907, and merged in 1910 to become **The National League For Opposing Women's Suffrage**

PART ONE

THE SUFFRAGETTE TIMELINE

The Suffragette Timeline

19th Century

The modernisation of Parliament began in 1832, but despite the widening of the male franchise, women remained specifically excluded from the vote. By the mid-1860s, women were beginning to organise, but were not yet able to put enough pressure on MPs to take their cause seriously. The last quarter of the century saw an increasing number of Parliamentarians attempting to expand the vote, but numerous opportunities to enfranchise women were rejected by the Establishment.

1817
Jeremy Bentham, social reformer, philosopher and jurist published his 'Plan of Parliamentary Reform', which included the call for individual and economic freedoms, the separation of church and state, freedom of expression, equal rights for women and the right to divorce.

7 June 1832
The 'Representation of the People Act' (informally known as The First Reform Act) carried out modernising reforms to Parliament including the abolition of 'Rotten Boroughs'. The electorate was increased but specifically excluded women from the franchise by using the term 'male person' in the legislation. While a woman could be vested with supreme authority (like Queen Victoria), no other woman could exercise even the simplest political function.

15 July 1858
Emmeline Pankhurst (nee Goulden) was born to politically active parents in Moss Side, Manchester.

March 1865
The Kensington Society, a suffrage discussion group which met in London, was formed. This group discussed women's rights and organised a campaign for female suffrage, education and property holding. In 1867, they became the London National Society for Women's Suffrage, eventually merging with the National Union of Women's Suffrage Societies (NUWSS).

Autumn of 1865
John Stuart Mill (political economist and utilitarian philosopher) was elected Liberal MP for Westminster and mentioned women's suffrage in his election address.

7 June 1866
John Stuart Mill became the first British politician in Parliament to formally take up the cause of women's suffrage when he presented an amendment to the 'Reform Bill', calling for a female franchise based on the property qualification. His efforts were sparked by a petition with 1,499 signatures prepared by the Kensington Society. The amendment was defeated by 196 votes to 73.

1867
The 'Second Reform Act' effectively doubled the electorate by giving the vote to around one million urban males. Backed by more women's petitions, John Stuart Mill attempted to move an amendment to insert the word 'person' instead of 'male person' into the Act, but was unable to gather enough support in Parliament.

6 November 1867
The National Society for Women's Suffrage, the first national group to campaign for votes for women, was founded in Manchester by Lydia Becker. Richard Pankhurst was also a member. An Edinburgh chapter of the society was formed soon after by Eliza Wigham.

14 April 1868
The Manchester National Society for Women's Suffrage held their first public meeting at Manchester Free Trade Hall. The Mayor of Salford took the Chair and the speakers were Lydia Becker, Anne Robinson and Agnes Pochin.

1869
John Stuart Mill's essay 'The Subjection of Women', made the case for perfect equality and argued that the oppression of women severely impeded the progress of humanity.

1869
'The Municipal Franchise Act', proposed by radical Liberal MP Jacob Bright, was passed by Parliament giving single women ratepayers the right to vote in local council elections. This act also enabled women to serve as Poor Law Guardians, which many did, including Emmeline Pankhurst in Manchester.

March 1870
The Women's Suffrage Journal was first published in Manchester and was edited by Lydia Becker.

The Suffragette Timeline

1871
Jacob Bright introduced the 'Women's Disabilities Removal Bill', drafted by Dr Richard Pankhurst, which passed its Second Reading in the House of Commons but fell after being opposed by the Government. The Bill was reintroduced by Bright in 1872 with the same result.

1877
Newly re-elected after a by-election in Manchester, pro-suffrage MP Jacob Bright introduced a 'Women's Suffrage Bill' without the married women exclusion clause, but it was again defeated.

31 January 1881
The Tynwald, the Parliament of the Isle of Man, became the first national Parliament to give women the right vote in a General Election, but it still excluded married women. In 1919, with the introduction of universal adult suffrage based on residency, women were able to stand for election.

1882
'The Married Women's Property Act' (building on earlier legislation in 1870) was passed, and altered the common law doctrine of coverture to include the wife's right to own, buy and sell property in her own name. Wives' legal identities were also restored, as the courts were forced to recognize a husband and a wife as two separate legal entities. The bill was drafted by lawyer Richard Pankhurst, who had married Emmeline Goulden, twenty-four years his junior, in 1878.

1884
'The Third Reform Act' was introduced by William Gladstone and extended the vote to all males paying over £10 per year in rent (or holding land worth more than £10). This increased the electorate to around 5.5 million, however 40% of men and all women were still not yet enfranchised.

12 June 1884
William Woodall MP, tried to introduce an amendment to the Act to include women, but was defeated. Mr Gladstone made a speech against the amendment, saying disparagingly about a woman's ability to understand political issues, *"The cargo which the vessel carries is, in our opinion, a cargo as large as she can safely carry."* This prompted Emmeline Pankhurst to describe him as *"an implacable foe of women's suffrage."*

3 November 1884
Mistresses of Dulwich School presented a petition to the House of Lords. It asked for the enfranchisement of 'duly qualified women' to be inserted in the 'Franchise Bill', which was then before Parliament. The petitioners argued that while two million of the least educated section of the population (for example agricultural and other labourers) would be added to the electorate, it was unjust to exclude 'educated and intelligent women who are heads of households.'

July 1888
Over 1400 women, working in appalling conditions at the Bryant And May match factory in Bow, East London, went on strike after one of them was unfairly sacked. With questions asked in Parliament, and widespread news coverage, this was one of the earliest examples of collective political and industrial action by women.

25 July 1889
The Woman's Franchise League, formed by Richard and Emmeline Pankhurst, held its inaugural meeting in London. Its radicalism was somewhat ahead of its time, and the group lost most of its members within a year.

18 July 1890
Lydia Becker, one of the most tireless campaigners for women's suffrage, died in France aged 63.

1892
Conservative MP for South Islington, Albert Rollit introduced another Private Member's Bill proposing women's suffrage for municipal workers, but was opposed by future Prime Minister Henry Herbert Asquith, and narrowly defeated.

28 November 1893
New Zealand became the first country in the World to give women equal voting rights with men.
The image of Kate Sheppard, the suffrage campaigner, was later added to their $10 Dollar note.

The next day, Elizabeth Yates became Mayor of Onehunga, the first time such a post had been held by a female anywhere in the British Empire.

The Suffragette Timeline

1894
The 'Local Government Act' extended the right to vote in municipal elections to some married women. By 1900, more than 1 million single women were registered to vote in local government elections in England, but still had no such right in Parliamentary elections.

1894
Emmeline Pankhurst was elected to the Board Of Poor Law Guardians of Chorlton in Manchester. Horrified by the degrading conditions suffered by women, children and the elderly, she became convinced that social change would not happen without women being granted the vote. She said *"I began to think about the vote in women's hands not only as a right but as a desperate necessity."*

1896
Scottish MP Ferdinand Faithful Begg introduced a 'Parliamentary Franchise (Extension to Women) Bill'. A special appeal had been launched in 1893 to involve women in the campaign, and this massive effort resulted in 257,796 signatures being collected from women all over Great Britain. However, with several other pieces of legislation on women's suffrage being considered, Begg's bill was not discussed.

3 February 1897
Begg came the closest yet to achieving some sort of women's franchise when his 'Bill For The Enfranchisement Of Women Householders' was actually passed in the House of Commons by a majority of seventy-one. The Bill was set down for committee stages to begin on 23 June, but when the time came four months later, opponents had got themselves organised and the Bill was talked out and made no further progress.

14 October 1897
Following the 1895 general election, the London, Manchester and other provincial women's groups merged form the National Union of Women's Suffrage Societies (NUWSS). United under the leadership of Millicent Fawcett, she remained the president of the society for more than twenty years. The organisation campaigned to achieve women's suffrage through peaceful and legal means, particularly by introducing Parliamentary Bills, and would later come into conflict with the more radical methods proposed by Emmeline Pankhurst and her Suffragette followers.

5 July 1898
Richard Pankhurst, died of stomach ulcers aged 62. Twenty four years older than his widow Emmeline, their daughters Christabel (1880-1958), Sylvia (1882-1960), and Adela (1885-1961) all became Suffragettes.

The Suffragette Timeline

1900-1905

The new century saw a number of fruitless constitutional attempts to change the law to introduce women's suffrage, but in reality, the lack of progress caused many women to lose faith in the political process. Under Lord Salisbury's government (1901-1905), there was almost no progress towards votes for women. It was this frustration that led Emmeline Pankhurst to form the Women's Social and Political Union (WSPU) in 1903, and immediately, she showed a willingness to start a campaign of direct action. By 1905, the women's movement was adopting increasingly militant language, and Christabel Pankhurst and Annie Kenney became the first Suffragettes to be jailed after disrupting a Liberal Party meeting in Manchester.

May 1900
The North of England Society for Women's Suffrage organised a working women's petition in favour of the vote.

1902
The suffrage pioneer Susan B. Anthony made a speech in Manchester, and Christabel Pankhurst, one of the many women inspired, said *"It is unendurable to think of another generation of women wasting their lives for the vote. We must not lose any more time. We must act."*

10 October 1903
Emmeline Pankhurst, disappointed by the Independent Labour Party's half-hearted support for the female franchise, founded the Women's Social and Political Union (WSPU) in her house in Nelson Street in Manchester. Membership was only open to women, and free from any overt party affiliation, the WSPU's declared aim was to obtain the vote for women on the same terms as men. Their motto was 'Deeds Not Words.'

3 February 1904
Mrs Pankhurst lobbied Parliament with members of other suffrage societies, but was disillusioned at what she saw was having to beg 'hypocritical politicians' to show up and support a Private Member's Bill.

This failure of Parliament and MPs to take the women's suffrage issue seriously hardened her resolve that action must be taken to force change.

1904
Christabel Pankhurst applied to Lincoln's Inn to study law but was refused because of her gender. She was later admitted to Manchester University where she gained a First Class Honours degree in law.

21 February 1905
Kier Hardie, the first MP elected for the Independent Labour Party (ILP), attempted to win a place for the reintroduction of a women's franchise bill, but despite lobbying of other MPs by Mrs Pankhurst, no Parliamentary slot was forthcoming. Eventually another MP yielded his place and the Bill was set down for 12 May. The WSPU collected signatures for a petition and lobbied the Easter ILP Conference to support the bill, while the NUWSS also held a meeting in its support.

12 May 1905
Women from many suffrage organisations packed the lobby of the House of Commons for the debate. Discussion of the preceding bill, about carriage lighting, was spun out leaving only half an hour for the 'Franchise Bill', which was duly talked out of time. The women attending were furious and followed Emmeline Pankhurst outside where she and veteran feminist campaigner, Mrs Wolstonholme Elmy, addressed the hundreds of indignant women. Police, wary of inflaming the mood, made no arrests. Mrs Pankhurst stated, *"This was the first militant act of the WSPU. It caused comment and even some alarm, but the police contented themselves with taking our names."*

13 October 1905
Christabel Pankhurst and Annie Kenney attended a meeting in the Free Trade Hall in Manchester where Liberal politician Sir Edward Grey was the main speaker. The Pankhursts had prepared a large banner which said 'Will the Liberal party give Votes For Women?', but they were unable to obtain seats with enough room to unfurl it. At the last minute, they cut it shorter and the simple words 'Votes For Women' became a slogan used by women suffragists all over the world.

The Suffragette Timeline

When their submission of a written question was ignored by the platform, Christabel and Annie rose to speak, but the male crowd turned on them, kicking, pushing and forcing them out of their seats. When they tried to address the crowds outside the Hall, they were promptly arrested.

14 October 1905
First Suffragette jail sentences
In court on the following day, Christabel was sentenced to a ten shilling fine or seven days in prison, and Annie to a five shilling fine or three days in prison. Both women chose to go to prison, which caused a storm of press debate over their tactics, and made them both household names.

5 December 1905
Conservative Prime Minister Arthur Balfour resigned and Henry Campbell-Bannerman, leader of the Liberal Party, formed a minority government pending a new general election.

21 December 1905
Three young activists for the WSPU disrupted a Liberal Party meeting at the Royal Albert Hall where Campbell-Bannerman was about to give his first speech as Prime Minister. Annie Kenney (a factory worker, already well known as an agitator) and Teresa Billington-Greig (a teacher) attended after the Labour MP Keir Hardie helped them to get tickets. Annie Kenney went in disguise, in a thick veil, dressed as a 'lady' with a maid (a new recruit from the East End whose identity remains unknown). In front of an audience of around 6,000 men, they rose to their feet to shout "Votes For Women" before unfurling a nine-foot-long banner behind the organ. They were quickly bundled out of the meeting, but this was to be the first in a decade of significant moments in Suffragette history at the Royal Albert Hall.

The Suffragette Timeline

1906 - 1907

The word 'Suffragette' was used for the first time in 1906. Originally a term of derision by journalists at the Daily Mail, it was proudly adopted by Mrs Pankhurst's WSPU (which had relocated to London) as a badge for someone who believed in militant action. It also became useful in drawing a dividing line between the militant Suffragettes and the non-militant constitutional Suffragists.

Despite a steady rise in the number of Parliamentary supporters, the Liberal Government made no practical moves to expand the franchise, and the first nationally reported demonstrations began in an attempt to put more pressure on MPs. By 1907, the Suffragettes' efforts were met with a rising tide of repression with the arrest and imprisonment of campaigners now became more regular.

January 1906
Throughout the General Election campaign, WSPU policy was now to oppose the Liberal Government by interrupting and disrupting their meetings and rallies. The election of 29 Labour MPs gave the campaign for the vote a significant Parliamentary boost.

19 February 1906
The WSPU held its first meeting in Caxton Hall, London, attended by 300-400 women, mainly from the East End of London where Annie Kenney had been campaigning. After learning, during the meeting, that the King's Speech contained no promise of votes for women, Emmeline Pankhurst led a deputation of women direct to the House of Commons. The police allowed only a handful to enter Parliament, as the rest of the crowd of women were kept outside in the rain. But Mrs Pankhurst saw it as a critical juncture in the campaign and said, *"...those woman had followed me to the House of Commons. They had defied the police. They were awake at last ... our militant movement was established."*

February 1906
Emmeline Pethick-Lawrence joined the WSPU as Treasurer of a completely empty bank account. The Union started to operate from the Pethick-Lawrence's flat at 4 Clement's Inn in London.

3 March 1906
Annie Kenney and Flora Drummond led a group of ten women to see Prime Minister Campbell-Bannerman. He was reportedly ill and refused to meet with them.

9 March 1906
After the Prime Minister recovered, Annie Kenney, Flora Drummond and Irene Miller led about thirty women to see the PM at his home – the press were waiting but he yet again refused to see them. Three women tried to gain entry to 10 Downing Street, and after a struggle with the police, they were arrested. Formal charges were dropped to avoid negative publicity.

25 April 1906
The Prime Minister announced he would receive a deputation of 200 MPs who had formed a Women's Suffrage Committee. Keir Hardie introduced a resolution in favour of votes for women and Emmeline, Christabel and Sylvia Pankhurst and other women supporters watched from behind the grille in the Ladies' Gallery in the House Of Commons as the debate began. A number of opposing MPs openly ridiculed the motion, with laughing and joking, and the angry women started a disturbance when it seemed the Resolution would be talked out. An order was given to clear the Gallery, but the women refused to leave, leading to an angry confrontation as they were dragged out by force. Members of the National Union of Women's Suffrage Societies (NUWSS) were appalled by the militant actions of the Pankhursts and their followers. This early disagreement about tactics would eventually lead to a schism between the two main women's suffrage groups

19 May 1906
A deputation of 350 women from twenty-five organisations marched from the statue of Boadicea (at the end of Westminster Bridge) to the Foreign Office to see the Prime Minister. Represented were women from the Independent Labour Party, Liberal Women's Associations, working women's groups and various other suffrage societies. The deputation was headed by Emily Davies, one of the two women who had handed the first very suffrage petition to Parliament in 1866. The Prime Minister congratulated the women on the way they had presented themselves but urged patience with the various reform efforts, in effect not promising anything at all. This was followed by a demonstration in Trafalgar Square, where speakers included Mrs Pankhurst, Keir Hardie and Mrs Wolstenholme Elmy.

The Suffragette Timeline

20 June 1906
Annie Kenney and three others were sentenced to between six-eight weeks in Holloway Prison for trying to force a their way into a meeting with the Chancellor of the Exchequer, Herbert Asquith.

Summer 1906
The word 'Suffragette' was first used, originally by the press as a term of derision, but was adopted enthusiastically by members of the WSPU as a way of differentiating themselves from the 'constitutionals' who became known as the Suffragists. These terms were to become very important in labelling the different groups of women over the next decade, campaigning for the same thing, but often by very different means.

October 1906
The WSPU opened its headquarters in Clement's Inn, London and began to step-up its anti-Government campaigning.

23 October 1906
A WSPU demonstration at the lobby of the House of Commons resulted in the arrest of ten women, including Annie Kenney and Emmeline Pethick-Lawrence, who were each sentenced to six weeks' imprisonment. Sylvia Pankhurst's protest at the trial resulted in fourteen days in prison for her. There were another four similar demonstrations by the end of the year.

27 October 1906
Millicent Fawcett wrote a letter to The Times supporting the action of the Suffragettes and laying the blame for their tactics with the Government for ignoring women's demands for so long.

24 November 1906
Millicent Fawcett arranged a welcome home dinner at the Savoy Hotel for the prisoners sent to jail the previous month.

31 December 1906
By the end of 1906, a total of forty-two women had been arrested and sentenced for demonstrating in various ways during the year.

9 February 1907
The National Union of Women's Suffrage Societies (NUWSS) organised the very first mass demonstration by women. The procession in London saw 3,000 women from all backgrounds walking through London from Hyde Park to Exeter Hall.

Unfortunately, the weather was awful and Millicent Fawcett said afterwards, *"The London weather did its worst against us; mud, mud, mud, was its prominent feature, and it was known among us afterwards as the 'mud march.'"* However, the number, organisation and dignity of the marchers showed the British public that women were serious in their demands.

13 February 1907
The day after Parliament opened, the WSPU held its own 'Women's Parliament' in Caxton and Exeter Halls, Westminster. The Suffragettes were angry that the King's Speech had yet again failed to mention women's suffrage for the next session of Parliament. Mrs Pankhurst proposed that they should march to see the Prime Minster and his cabinet and when the shout from the platform came of *"Rise Up Women"* the answer was a resounding *"YES!"*

The women were organised into ranks and sang as they marched. When they reached Abbey Green in front of Parliament they were met with a cordon of mounted police and scuffling broke out. Over fifty women were arrested, including the elderly but indomitable Charlotte Despard, Christabel and Sylvia Pankhurst. When the Magistrate charged Christabel the next day he said, *"These disorderly scenes in the streets must be stopped."* Christabel replied, *"They can be, but only in one way. One thing is certain, there can be no going back for us and more will happen if we don't get justice."*

All the women refused to pay the fines and chose to go to jail, leading to the Daily Mirror declaring 'Holloway is full up.'

14 February 1907
All women were banned from Central Lobby at the Palace of Westminster, unless accompanied by an MP. Women had previously been allowed to protest there, although many of them had been blacklisted. This ban was enforced until 1918.

19 March 1907
Mr Dickinson, the Liberal MP for North St Pancras, reintroduced his 'Women's Suffrage Bill' but it was talked out at its Second Reading.

One MP, a Mr Rees, made jokes about the embarrassment which the presence of ladies in the House may cause. This time, there were no interruptions from the Ladies' Gallery as it had been closed.

The Suffragette Timeline

20 March 1907
Following the failure of Mr Dickinson's Bill, a second Women's Parliament was held in Caxton Hall. The Suffragettes hoped to sneak into Parliament by dressing up as 'Lancashire Lassies'. A full-scale battle with the Police erupted as women tried to gain entry, and ended with seventy-five women under arrest.

Summer 1907
The Suffragettes campaigned over the Summer at various By-Elections gathering support for their cause and working against the Liberal Party candidates.

October 1907
Concerns in the WSPU about the Pankhurst's autocratic governing style led to the formation of a splinter organisation, the Women's Freedom League, although the WFL retained WSPU policy and continued using militant but non-violent methods.

October 1907
Mr and Mrs Pethick-Lawrence launched the 'Votes for Women' newspaper as the official voice of the Women's Social and Political Union. Starting as a monthly, it contained articles by the Pethick-Lawrences, features on policy by Christabel, and a history of the organisation by Sylvia.

The Suffragette Timeline

1908

Militancy by the Suffragettes reached a new level, with mass demonstrations, and the first real acts of violence in support of the campaign. The number of arrests gradually increased and both Emmeline and Christabel were imprisoned in Holloway. The women's movement began to split, with increasing numbers of Suffragists outraged by the militancy of the WSPU. However, by the end of the year, the pressure had begun to tell, with the Liberal Government, at long last, opening the door to some change.

30 January 1908
Herbert Henry Asquith, about to become leader of the Liberal Party, told a deputation from the NUWSS that the Government would not introduce a bill for women's suffrage or allow facilities for a Private Member's Bill. He replaced Campbell-Bannerman as Prime Minister in April 1908.

11 February 1908
The first day of a three-day WSPU Women's Parliament session ended in a deputation to Parliament from Caxton Hall. Henry Pankhurst (Emmeline's son) devised the idea of a Trojan Horse to deliver a group of Suffragettes straight into the heart of Westminster in two furniture vans. They were 'delivered' to the House of Commons and tried to rush into St Stephen's entrance. Two women succeeded into getting inside, but were arrested and sentenced to terms in prison.

13 February 1908
Mrs Pankhurst challenged an ancient statute of Charles II, under which more than twelve people approaching Parliament or the King could be imprisoned, by (provocatively) leading a deputation of thirteen women. She and eight other women were arrested and sentenced to six weeks' imprisonment.

28 February 1908
A Private Member's Bill in favour of women's suffrage, brought by Liberal MP H.Y. Stanger, was carried at its Second Reading by 271 votes to 92, but its further progress was blocked by the Speaker, by referring it to a committee of the whole House.

19 March 1908
The WSPU held its first meeting at the Royal Albert Hall in Kensington, the largest meeting hall in London which could seat up to 10,000 people. Although Mrs Pankhurst had been in jail since February, an empty chair was symbolically placed on the stage. However, on her early release, she made her way to the meeting. In her autobiography she described what happened next:

"My release was not expected until the following morning, and no one thought of my appearing at the meeting. My chairman's seat was decorated with a large placard with the inscription, 'Mrs Pankhurst's Chair'. After all the others were seated, the speakers, and hundreds of ex-prisoners, I walked quietly onto the stage, took the placard out of the chair and sat down. A great cry went up from the women as they sprang from their seats and stretched their hands towards me. It was some time before I could see them for my tears, or speak to them for the emotion that shook me like a storm."

5 April 1908
Herbert Asquith became Prime Minister, and as an avowed anti-suffragist, his Government was not welcomed by the suffrage movement. Mrs Pankhurst said, *"It was sufficiently plain to us that no methods of education or persuasion would ever prove successful as far as he was concerned. Therefore, the necessity of action on our part was greater than ever."*

Mid May 1908
In preparation for the first big demonstration of the year planned for June, Emmeline Pethick-Lawrence, (Treasurer of the WSPU and co-editor of 'Votes for Women') introduced the Suffragette colours of purple, white and green. Purple represented loyalty and dignity, white for purity, and green was for hope. Members were encouraged to wear the colours 'as a duty and a privilege.' WSPU shops sprang up around the country selling ribbons, badges, hats and rosettes. Selfridges and Liberty even sold underwear, handbags, shoes, slippers and toilet soap in Suffragette colours.

20 May 1908
Prime Minister Asquith told a deputation of sixty Liberal MPs that he would not consider Mr Stanger's bill, but offered to bring in electoral reform before the end of the Parliament.

The Suffragette Timeline

Many campaigners speculated that female franchise would be included, but the WSPU remained highly sceptical that the Government could be trusted. During the debate Herbert Gladstone patronisingly questioned whether women would be able to organise mass demonstrations as the Chartists had done, and the women's suffrage societies determined to prove him wrong.

13 June 1908
The NUWSS held a procession of 13,000 women from the Embankment to the Royal Albert Hall. Speakers include Millicent Fawcett, Lady Frances Balfour, Lady Henry Somerset, Dr Anna Shaw (of Philadelphia), Charlotte Despard (President of the Women's Freedom League) and Mrs Hodgett (President of the Co-Operative Guild).

21 June 1908
The WSPU organised a massive demonstration in Hyde Park, London. It took four months to plan and extra trains were organised to bring supporters from the suburbs, advertising hoardings went up around the UK and even cinema advertising was used to inform women about the event.
On a hot and sunny day, the event featured over eighty women speakers on twenty platforms distributed around the park. It was attended by Thomas Hardy, H G Wells and George Bernard Shaw and some estimates put the crowds at double the expected 250,000.
This was also the first time that the Suffragette colours (purple, white and green) had been seen and soon ribbons, scarves and sashes in the Suffragette colours were flying off the shelves.
At 5 o'clock precisely there was to be a 'Great Shout' - when all the women in the whole of Hyde Park cried out *"VOTES FOR WOMEN, VOTES FOR WOMEN, VOTES FOR WOMEN."*
After the meeting, Christabel Pankhurst sent its resolution to Asquith asking for his response to so large a gathering. He replied that he had nothing to add to his statement of 20 May. In response the WSPU called for a public meeting in Parliament Square nine days later.

30 June 1908
First acts of criminal damage
Huge crowds gathered once again for this meeting. The women met at Caxton Hall and a delegation of twelve, led by Mrs Pankhurst, set out for the House of Commons.

The Prime Minister refused to see them, so Mrs Pankhurst returned to Caxton Hall and urged the waiting women to march to Parliament Square to protest. As the women tried to gain entrance to the Palace of Westminster, the crowd became rowdy and the police reacted by arresting thirty women. The demonstrators were treated with such brutality by the police and men in the crowd that two women incensed by the violence, went to Downing Street and threw stones at the Prime Minister's windows. This was the first serious act of damage by Suffragettes, Mrs Pankhurst endorsed their actions, and Mary Leigh and Edith New each received two months in prison for window smashing.

21 July 1908
The Women's Anti-Suffrage League was formed, arguing that the influence of women in social causes would be diminished rather than increased by the possession of the Parliamentary vote. A petition of over 330,000 signatures was collected to demonstrate that not all women were in favour of enfranchisement.

September 1908
Mrs Pankhurst, Christabel and Flora Drummond issued an inflammatory leaflet urging members of the public to support direct action. It read, 'Men and Women, Help the Suffragettes rush the House Of Commons on Tuesday Evening, October 13th at 7.30'

11 October 1908
A large rally was held in Trafalgar Square, where Mrs Pankhurst, Christabel and Flora addressed the crowds.

12 October 1908
The police discovered a copy of the September leaflet and Emmeline and Christabel Pankhurst and Mrs Drummond were served with a summons to appear at Bow Street Police Station.

13 October 1908
The three leaders refused to hand themselves in until the evening of the 13th, by which another demonstration was underway in Parliament Square.

21 October 1908
At her trial for inciting the 'rush' on Parliament, Christabel Pankhurst was able to use her law qualification when she cross-examined David Lloyd George (Chancellor of the Exchequer) and Herbert Gladstone (Home Secretary), who she had called as witnesses. Despite a number of witnesses who testified the demonstration was orderly, she was eventually sentenced to ten weeks in prison. Mrs Pankhurst and Flora Drummond were each sentenced to three months. The WSPU held processions and protest rallies outside Holloway during their incarceration.

28 October 1908
Two members of the Women's Freedom League, Helen Fox and Australian Muriel Matters chained themselves to the grille in the Ladies' Gallery in the House of Commons. The padlocks could not be undone and the authorities had to remove the whole grille with the women still attached. The NUWSS executive now repudiated all militant action. Women were not allowed back into the main visitor's gallery until 1918.

29 October 1908
A WSPU meeting at the Royal Albert Hall was to have been presided over by Mrs Pankhurst but following her imprisonment the previous Saturday, the meeting was chaired by Emmeline Pethick-Lawrence. At the back of the stage a large banner displayed the words 'Neither to Change, Nor Falter, Nor Repent - Mrs Pankhurst, Christabel Pankhurst, Mrs Drummond. Imprisoned Oct 21st 1908'. The publicity generated for the campaign was hugely successful, and raised £3,000 for the WSPU war chest.

3 November 1908
Mrs Drummond was released on the grounds of ill health, but was able to organise a huge demonstration of women dressed in prison uniform, which marched from Kingsway to Holloway. The procession was a mile and a half long with brass bands and thousands of supporters. When they reached Holloway the bands played and the procession circled the prison twice before shouting *"Three cheers for Mrs Pankhurst,"* and returning to Clement's Inn.

18 November 1908
Women in Australia got the right to vote, although indigenous women had to wait until 1962.

5 December 1908

Lloyd George, having offered to address a Women's Liberal Federation meeting about votes for women at the Royal Albert Hall, was heckled by Suffragettes in prison dress. One of the WSPU contingent defended herself from an assault by a steward with a dog whip; an Evening Standard reporter later protested about the 'grossly brutal conduct' of the stewards. As a result of the publicity, Lloyd George excluded all women from his future meetings.

22 December 1908

Thousands of people gathered to greet Emmeline and Christabel Pankhurst, and Mrs Leigh as they were released from Holloway. They travelled to Queen's Hall for a celebration breakfast where Mrs Pankhurst made this passionate speech:

"When men begin an agitation like ours, they are of course open to all kinds of criticism and attack, but I do not think that the very dangerous and difficult form of attack is brought to bear against them that is brought to bear against us. Men are never told that they are hysterical, and that they do not know what they are doing. They may be told they are violent , they may be told their action is reprehensible, but people are usually willing to admit that at least there is method in their madness."

The Suffragette Timeline

1909

This was a year of great upheaval and challenge for the women's suffrage movement. Determined not to be treated as common criminals, the Suffragettes began hunger-striking, and the brutal Government response of forcible feeding sent shockwaves around Britain, and forced the Suffragettes into increasing levels of militancy and violence.
The year also saw the introduction of two new women's suffrage publications. In April the National Union of Women's Suffrage Societies launched 'The Common Cause' and in October, the Freedom League issued 'The Vote'.

14 January 1909
Mrs Pankhurst was presented with a special necklace of amethysts, pearls and emeralds (the Suffragette colours) as a thank you present from the WSPU at a special meeting at the Queen's Hall. This meeting was held to welcome her and Mrs Leigh home, after their recent prison sentences.

19 January 1909
Christabel Pankhurst was given a rousing reception at Manchester's Free Trade Hall. Her co-speaker, Miss Gawthorpe, declared that the Government had been trying to side-track the issue of votes for women for forty years and urged that women put up with this no longer. Christabel defended the militant methods adopted by the WSPU, demanded action from politicians, and asserted, *"We tried to rush the House of Commons and we might have to do it again."*

25 January 1909
Hearing that Asquith was receiving various deputations, the WSPU decided to send one of their own to the first Cabinet meeting of the year. However, for committing the crime of simply knocking on the front door of 10 Downing street, four women (including Mrs Pankhurst's sister Mary Clarke) were arrested and eventually sentenced to one month in prison.

16 February 1909
Australian Suffragette Muriel Matters (who had achieved notoriety the previous year for chaining herself up in the Houses of Parliament) hired a hot air balloon to fly over Westminster as the King opened Parliament.

'Votes For Women' was painted on the balloon, and although she planned to drop leaflets over London, she was blown off course and eventually landed in a field in Surrey. Nevertheless, her stunt made headlines around the World.

24 February 1909
The Sixth Women's Parliament met at Caxton Hall and another deputation to the House of Commons was greeted with the usual brutality. Twenty-eight women were arrested and sent to jail, including Emmeline Pethick-Lawrence and Lady Constance Lytton.

24 March 1909
A special welcome home dinner was held for the woman arrested in February.

March 1909
Geoffrey Howard (Private Secretary to Asquith) introduced a Private Members' Bill to expand the vote, but was opposed by all suffrage societies who did not think votes for women should be an after-thought to an extension of the male franchise. Prime Minister Asquith declared that such important legislation should be a Government measure and voted against it. Although the Bill was carried by thirty-four votes, the Government still refused to allow further time for discussion.

30 March 1909
After the Seventh Women's Parliament twenty-one women were arrested. Another Private Members' Bill to introduce limited suffrage (on a three-month residential qualification) was again opposed by all suffrage societies, as not going far enough.

17 April 1909
The Aldwych Theatre in London's West End was hired for a meeting to welcome home Emmeline Pethick-Lawrence from Holloway. Elsie Howey, a member of the WSPU dressed as Joan of Arc, (Mrs Pethick-Lawrence's favourite character from history) and she was also presented with a car painted in the Suffragette colours of green, white and purple.

27 April 1909
Four members of the WSPU, (Margery Humes, Theresa Garnet, Sylvia Russell and Bertha Quinn) chained themselves to the statues in the entrance to the House of Commons to help advertise a rally at the Royal Albert Hall.

The four women who were waiting in St Stephen's Hall, supposedly to meet MPs, suddenly revealed the steel chains they had concealed under their cloaks and attached themselves to four statues, shouting, *"Votes for women… We will have the vote and nothing you can do will stop us."* In the subsequent struggle to cut the chains and remove the women, the spur of Viscount Falkland's boot was snapped off, and there is now a small brass plaque on the statue to tell the story, as the spur has never been repaired.

27 April 1909
In a rally organised by the NUWSS, over 1,000 women representing a pageant of women's trades and professions including teachers, doctors, journalists, actresses, and pit workers, marched to the Royal Albert Hall, carrying banners and 500 lanterns to light the way. Simultaneously, the Suffragist International Congress was being held in London. Speakers at the Hall were Millicent Fawcett and Ramsay MacDonald MP (who would become Labour's first Prime Minister in 1924). It was reported: 'Mr Ramsay MacDonald MP moved a resolution expressing satisfaction with the progress of the women's suffrage movement. The resolution was carried by acclamation.'

29 April 1909
At a WSPU meeting at the Royal Albert Hall, members who had been to prison were presented with a distinctive 'Holloway broach' and certificate, designed by Sylvia Pankhurst.
(See the article in Suffragette Stories)

9 May 1909
Thousands of American women marched in Washington DC to the Senate to demand 'Votes for Women'. Five thousand women massed around the East Steps of the Capitol singing Ethel Smyth's 'March of the Women'. Although many of the United States had already passed laws granting women's suffrage, it did not become part of the constitution of the United States until 4 June 1920. However, within a decade, state laws and vigilante intimidation effectively disenfranchised most black women in the South. It was not until the Civil Rights Movement of the 1960s, that these black women would be allowed to vote.

9-25 May 1909
The WSPU hired the Prince's Skating Rink in Knightsbridge for an ambitious fund-raising event. The Pethick-Lawrences planned the event and Sylvia Pankhurst was asked to design the posters and interior decorations.

She employed ex-students from the Royal College of Art (where she had studied) to help her complete the massive canvases and wall hangings for the event. A Suffragette drum and fife band, led by Mary Leigh and dressed in smart uniforms in the Suffragette colours marched from Kingsway to Knightsbridge to advertise the celebration. Fund-raising stalls sold sweets and hats and an ice cream soda fountain (the first ever seen in Britain) was paid for by a wealthy American supporter. The Exhibition raised a very healthy £5,644 for the WSPU coffers.

24 June 1909
First hunger-strike
Marion Wallace-Dunlop, an artist, disguised herself and entered Parliament with a male companion. Seated in St Stephen's Hall, she managed to stencil the date of the next women's deputation (29 June) and an extract from the Bill of Rights of 1689 before anyone noticed. In purple ink she stamped the words 'It is the right of the Subjects to petition the King and all commitments and prosecutions for such petitioning are illegal.' Charged and imprisoned, she became the first Suffragette to refuse food, and was released after ninety-one hours of hunger-striking.

29 June 1909
First organised act of window smashing
The eighth Women's Parliament saw a violent attack on demonstrators, and led to the WSPU's first official act of window breaking, causing damage to several Government buildings. 108 women were arrested and all the stone throwers were remanded in custody. Mrs Pankhurst and the women on the deputations pleaded that their action was within the Bill of Rights and their case was referred to the High Court to be tried in December. The stone throwers are sent to Holloway, where they smashed more windows and joined Marion Wallace-Dunlop on hunger strike.

5 July - 28 October 1909
Mrs Pankhurst agreed not to send any more deputations to Parliament pending the High Court hearing, but when Asquith refused to meet them, the Women's Freedom League set up a picket at the House of Commons. It lasted almost four months until 28 October.

17 August 1909
This week saw the appearance of Emmeline Pankhurst's first chauffeur, Vera 'Jack' Holme.

Mrs Pankhurst had been given a car for official business by the WSPU and the new Austin was painted and upholstered in the official Suffragette colours, with a green body, a purple stripe and white wheels! Vera was a fascinating and courageous woman who was an actress, lesbian and a militant Suffragette. (See the article in Suffragette Stories)

13 September 1909
Scottish Suffragette, Isabel Kelley, lowered herself twenty-five feet to disturb the meeting of Liberal Cabinet minister, Herbert Samuel at Dundee's Kinnaird Hall. The Liberals had already banned all women from their events, but they had not counted on the sheer determination of women like Isabel Kelley, who hid for seventeen hours on the roof of the building before making her protest. She was the only woman to successfully enter the Hall but was arrested before her protest could be made. Other women protesting outside were also arrested. Three Suffragettes, Alice Paul, Edith New and Lucy Burns refused to pay their fines and were sent to jail where they immediately began a hunger-strike.

17 September 1909
Asquith attempted to address a meeting at Bingley Hall in Birmingham. The hall was surrounded by police and women were banned from the meeting. However, earlier that day, two Suffragettes Mary Leigh and Charlotte Marsh, had climbed onto the roof of a neighbouring factory and had equipped themselves with axes. During the meeting they chopped slates from the roof and threw them down at Asquith's motor car. At least twenty men in the audience also disrupted the meeting in support of the cause. Fire hoses were turned on the two women but they still refused to surrender. Eventually police climbed onto the roof and brought the women down, soaked, bleeding and exhausted. There were other protests and before Asquith's train left Birmingham, iron bars and stones were thrown at one of the carriage windows. Eight more women are arrested, and Leigh and Marsh were imprisoned with hard labour for four and three months respectively. The other women got fourteen to twenty-eight days. In Winson Green Prison they went on hunger-strike. By this time, thirty-seven women had been released from prison on health grounds after hunger-striking. However, the Government was growing tired of being forced to terminate these prison sentences and the Home Secretary ordered their forcible feeding.

24 September 1909
Start of forcible feeding
The terrible news reached the outside world that the first hunger-striking Suffragettes in Winson Green had been forcibly fed. Mrs Pankhurst rushed to a meeting at the Temperance Hall in Birmingham to protest against this brutal new escalation of the Government's treatment of Suffragette prisoners. The crowds were huge and an overflow meeting was held in the Bull Ring, where Christabel Pankhurst held a reception.

Until this point the Government had released hunger-striking Suffragettes but this was a drastic change of policy and one that shocked the world. Emmeline and Christabel Pankhurst started legal proceedings against the Government. The 'Votes for Women' newspaper asked: 'Do they think that by these abominable means they are going to crush down the women's movement? If they think that, they prove once more how utterly they fail to understand the nature and determination of women.' Nevertheless, this barbaric method of torture was forced upon hundreds of women over the next five years, some of them being force fed on numerous occasions.

27 September 1909
Keir Hardie MP asked questions in the House about the truth of the force feeding of the Suffragettes in Winson Green and enquired about the health of Mary Leigh and Charlotte Marsh. It was confirmed that they had been force fed with the approval of the Home Secretary. Hardie asked further questions about this on the 29th September and 1st October.

28 September 1909
116 British Doctors signed a letter to the Home Secretary protesting at the forcible feeding in Winson Green. One Doctor with a Harley Street practice wrote, 'I consider that forcible feeding by the methods employed is an act of brutality beyond common endurance, and I am astounded that is it possible for Members of Parliament, with mothers, wives and sisters of their own, to allow it, however wrong the methods of the women may be.'

4 October 1909
Three University Graduates of Manchester University (Mary Gawthorpe, Dora Marsden BA and Rona Robinson MSc) dared to question Cabinet Minister Lord Morley, about the Suffragette prisoners in Birmingham being forcibly fed.

The Press reported that the women were ejected with great violence and arrested upon a charge of disorderly behaviour. The point was also made that questions and heckling from male graduates were welcomed as a sign of intellectual development but questions from women were not - even women who had graduated from that University!

5 October 1909
Laura Ainsworth became the first prisoner to be released from Winson Green after force feeding.

7 October 1909
A WSPU gathering at the Royal Albert Hall, described as an 'Indignation meeting', saw speeches from Emmeline Pethick-Lawrence and Mrs Pankhurst. Over £2,300 was raised at this meeting, and as the original £50,000 target had been reached, a new target of £100,000 was announced. The meeting passed the following defiant resolution:

'This meeting expresses its profound indignation of the recent disgraceful development of the Governments' policy of coercion against women and warns the Government that repression will rouse women into more determined rebellion, while only the concession of the vote to duly qualified women will bring this struggle to an end.'

9 October 1909
Scottish Suffragettes led by Flora Drummond organised the biggest Suffragette march Scotland had ever seen. Sometimes known as the 'Gude Cause' March, most of Edinburgh turned out to see thousands of women marching in the Suffragette colours. They marched from Bruntsfield Links down Lothian Road and along Princes Street, and spectators lined the road ten-deep, cramming balconies along the route. 'General' Flora Drummond sat astride a white horse leading the women from all classes and all industries through the streets of the City.

11 October 1909
A meeting was held in the Sun Hall, Liverpool where Mrs Pankhurst and various hunger-strikers spoke. The campaign was now becoming truly national.

13 October 1909
Mrs Pankhurst travelled to America to carry out a lecture tour. Arriving on 20 October, her new audience were shocked to see that a small and frail woman had caused such an uproar in Britain. Five days later, she spoke before a sell-out crowd in New York's Carnegie Hall.

28 October 1909
Emily Wilding Davison suffered an horrific ordeal in Strangeways Prison in Manchester, where she had been sentenced after smashing a window in the town. After being forcibly fed for several days, Emily could stand it no longer and barricaded herself into her cell. The prison authorities decided to smash the cell window and turned a hosepipe on Emily until she nearly lost consciousness. She was taken to the hospital wing where they continued to forcibly feed her until her release three days later. When she left the prison, she was shocked to find that the hosepipe incident was famous and questions were even asked about her in Parliament.
'Votes for Women' reported, 'Emily Wilding Davison attained on Thursday last, October 28, the triumph of the spirit over physical force. This day should be henceforth a red-letter day in the annals of the Union.'

October 1909
The Women's Tax Resistance League was formed. It was independent of other suffrage societies and based on the principle of 'No taxation without representation'. Women who refused to pay their taxes faced the seizure and sale of their property.

19 November 1909
Arriving at Bristol Station on his way to a meeting at Colston Hall, Winston Churchill was attacked with a riding whip by Theresa Garnet, who was later sentenced to a month in prison.

9 December 1909
The WSPU held a demonstration at the Royal Albert Hall at which Mrs Pankhurst received an enthusiastic welcome from a large audience on her return from America. Above the organ a banner was hung with the words 'No surrender.' The meeting also included a surprise appearance by Mary Leigh, just released from Winson Green Prison, and one of the first hunger-striking prisoners to be force fed.

She took legal action against the Home Secretary, Mr Gladstone, and the Governor and Doctor of Winson Green for 'having caused her to be fed by force, without her consent, and against her determined opposition and resistance.' Unfortunately, the judge and jury ruled against Mary Leigh and whenever the Suffragette prisoners were forcibly fed in the next five years, the case of 'Leigh vs. Gladstone' was cited to prove the legality of the practice.

10 December 1909
Jessie (Annie's sister) Kenney was discovered trying to gain admittance, disguised as a messenger boy, to a Liberal Party meeting at the Royal Albert Hall. Fearing constant disruption, the Liberal Party had banned all women from attending their meetings

December 1909
Selina Martin was arrested for breaking a window in Asquith's car in Liverpool. While on remand, she was force fed and pushed down some stairs while handcuffed in Walton Jail. Gladstone denied all the allegations.

December 1909
Harry Pankhurst died aged 20, after suffering from Polio. Emmeline Pankhurst was devastated by the loss of her youngest son.

The Suffragette Timeline

1910

The first half of the year saw a reduction in violence as hopes were pinned on progress towards a constitutional settlement in Parliament. However, the year ended with the most violent action of the campaign, on 'Black Friday', which led to the first deaths of Suffragettes from injuries received from police brutality and forcible feeding of hunger strikers.

January 1910
Asquith called a General Election. With hope that a new Government might bring change, the WSPU suspended militancy during the election, but actively campaigned in forty constituencies. The Liberals returned to power but with their previous majority swept away. After the election, H. N. Brailsford established an all-party 'Conciliation Committee' of MPs to draft a Bill, under the chairmanship of Lord Lytton, brother of prominent Suffragette Lady Constance Lytton.

14 January 1910
Lady Constance Lytton was the most aristocratic member of the WSPU and incredibly committed to the Union. She had been sentenced to prison for militant activities in 1909, but had always been treated very well and sent straight home because of her position in society. Constance was aware that many working class women in the Union were treated with brutality and contempt, so in January 1910, she disguised herself as a seamstress named Jane Wharton, cutting her hair, putting on spectacles and changing her clothes and boots. She travelled to Liverpool where she had heard reports that Suffragettes had been forcibly fed even while on remand. She joined a demonstration where she feebly tried to throw some stones, before she was arrested and sent to Walton Jail. She immediately went on hunger-strike and was force fed eight times in the month before her true identity was revealed. She was badly hurt by her ordeal and suffered from life-long health problems, which contributed to her early death at the age of fifty-four. However, she wrote eloquently of her ordeal in prison, which led to changes in how women prisoners were treated.

14 February 1910
The WSPU and WFL declared a 'truce' from militancy for the week before the opening of the new Parliament on 21 February. After a brutal few months, many Suffragettes were exhausted and hopeful that some positive publicity would accompany the reduction of violence.

18 March 1910
The WSPU held a meeting at the Royal Albert Hall. Speakers included Emmeline and Christabel Pankhurst, Mrs Pethick-Lawrence and a member of the Norwegian Parliament which had already given women the vote. The 'Medal for Valour' was presented to several women, including Lady Constance Lytton, who had suffered forcible feeding in Walton Jail.

6 May 1910
King Edward VII died, and all WSPU propaganda stopped until after the funeral.

14 June 1910
The 'Conciliation Bill' was introduced, which proposed the enfranchisement of women householders and women occupiers of business premises with a rateable value of £10 per annum and over. The WSPU formally extended the truce, but various suffrage societies demonstrated in support of the Bill by sending deputations to Prime Minister Asquith, who also received representations from anti-suffrage groups.

18 June 1910
In a spirit of optimism, the WSPU organised The Women's Suffrage procession marched from the Embankment to the Royal Albert Hall. The procession was 10,000 strong and organised in 130 contingents, designed to illustrate the theme 'From Prison to Citizenship'. After the 'Marseillaise' was sung by the audience, Mrs Pankhurst, introduced Lord Lytton (Chairman of the Woman Suffrage Conciliation Committee), Mrs Pethick-Lawrence, Christabel Pankhurst, and Annie Kenney. A resolution urging the Government to grant facilities to the Bill now before Parliament was put to the meeting.

21 June 1910
The Liberal Women's Suffrage Deputation was allowed in to see Asquith to ask for an early Second Reading of the 'Conciliation Bill', but the Prime Minister refused to promise any concessions.

The Suffragette Timeline

12 July 1910
The 'Conciliation Bill' passed its Second Reading by a majority of 110 votes.

13 July 1910
The WSPU held a demonstration in Hyde Park which welcomed the result, and called on the Government to provide facilities to enable the Bill to become law. However, Asquith refused to allow Government support, effectively killing any chance of a change in the law.

10 November 1910
At a meeting in the Royal Albert Hall, Mrs Pankhurst announced that a WSPU deputation would be sent in eight days' time as a last constitutional effort to secure the passage of the 'Conciliation Bill'. She stated, *"If the Bill is killed by the Government then I have to say there is an end to the truce."*

11 November 1910
Asquith went to Sandringham to visit the King, prompting fears that Parliament may be disbanded before the 'Conciliation Bill' could make any more progress.

12 November 1910
The NUWSS held a 'Suffrage Week' mass meeting at the Royal Albert Hall in an attempt to unite all the various campaigning groups in support of the 'Conciliation Bill'. Chaired by Millicent Fawcett, speakers came from a wide range of groups, demonstrating how support was growing across the country.

18 November 1910
'Black Friday'
On the day that Parliament reconvened, the WSPU held its ninth Women's Parliament. On learning that Asquith had not given Parliamentary time to the 'Conciliation Bill', (but agreeing to make a further statement on the matter), a deputation was sent to the House of Commons.
The police brutality that followed was so extreme that this day became known as 'Black Friday', with over one hundred women arrested. Mrs Pankhurst's sister Mary Clarke and Henrietta Williams sustained life-threatening injuries, during violent clashes with the police. Many of the reported assaults on the women were sexual in nature with many women complaining afterwards of attacks on the breasts such as nipping, wringing, pinching and twisting designed to cause the most humiliation. (see the article in Suffragette Stories)

22 November 1910
The Women's Parliament was still in session when Asquith's statement on the suffrage question was received. Once again, it failed to satisfy the WSPU and Mrs Pankhurst led another deputation to Downing Street; she and over one hundred other women are arrested. The next day another attempt to reach the House of Commons resulted in eighteen more arrests.

24 November 1910
Further window smashing resulted in twenty-one more arrests.

7 December 1910
A new Anti-Suffrage organisation was formed. The Women's National Anti-Suffrage League joined with The Men's League for Opposing Woman Suffrage to form the National League for Opposing Woman Suffrage. Lord Cromer became President, Lady Jersey was appointed Deputy President with Mr J Massie as Hon Treasurer.

7 December 1910
Twenty-six women who had been sentenced to fourteen days imprisonment for their 'raid' on the House of Commons were released from Holloway to a breakfast at the Criterion Restaurant with 250 WSPU supporters.

25 December 1910
Mary Jane Clarke died following injuries she sustained during force feeding in Holloway, where she had been sent after throwing stones on 'Black Friday'.
(See the article in Suffragette Stories)

29 December 1910
The low-key funeral of Mary Jane Clarke took place.

1911

This year saw a general reduction in violence, the Government at last seemed willing to take expansion of the franchise seriously. However, suspicion remained that giving the votes to more men, would be used as a diversionary tactic to resist the demands of women. WSPU militancy declined, in the hope that the Government would act, but by the end of the year, they became increasingly convinced that they were being betrayed by the Establishment once again.

1 January 1911
Miss Henrietta Williams, an active member the WSPU, died of her injuries sustained from the events of 'Black Friday' where she was 'gripped around the heart' by a policeman until she almost passed out. She never recovered from her injuries and died alone in her house in Upminster. She was buried a few days later in Glasgow's Cathcart Cemetery with members of the Glasgow WSPU attending and bouquets of flowers in the colours of green, white and purple.

3 January 1911
Suffragettes in Brighton held a special memorial service for Mary Jane Clarke, younger sister of Emmeline Pankhurst who died on Christmas Day, as a result of her injuries only two days after being released from Holloway.

15 January - 10 February 1911
Asquith was returned to Downing Street after the general election, with voting taking place over several weeks. The Liberal Party retained power in a minority Government supported by the Irish Parliamentary Party. Labour increased its MPs from twenty-nine to forty. The WSPU renewed its truce in the hope that the 'Conciliation Bill' would proceed at last.

21 January 1911
Suffragette and composer Dr. Ethel Smyth presented Mrs Pankhurst with her newly composed song 'March of the Women'. This became the rallying song of the militant Suffragettes, and Ethel Smyth declared at the meeting, *"If I have got into my music some of the quality that makes this the finest movement in the world, I will have done something"*.

23 March 1911
At a WSPU Meeting at the Royal Albert Hall, Ethel Smyth's 'March of the Women', the Suffragette anthem was launched. Cicely Hamilton, another Suffragette, wrote the lyrics and a choir of Suffragettes sang, having been rehearsed for weeks by Smyth. Smyth was presented with a ceremonial baton by Mrs Pankhurst, and proceeded to conduct the whole gathering in a mass rendition.

2 April 1911
Boycott of the census
Thousands of women across Britain hid from the authorities to avoid being counted in the 1911 Census. The idea was that if women could not vote, they would not cooperate with the Government by being counted. In cities all across Britain, women gathered in secret 'safe' houses to avoid the count, while in London, some Suffragettes hired the Aldwych skating rink so that they could skate through the night. In Wimbledon, some women took to horse drawn carriages for a secret night time trek. Women were encouraged to deface their census returns which they did in their hundreds. The most famous act of defiance on census night was by Emily Wilding Davison, who hid in a cupboard at the Houses of Parliament, later commemorated by a plaque placed there by Labour MP Tony Benn.

5 May 1911
An amended 'Conciliation Bill' passed its Second Reading. This led to a great feeling of optimism, and membership of suffrage societies surged.

29 May 1911
The Government promised that time would be given in the next Parliamentary session for the consideration of the 'Conciliation Bill', with the opportunity for further amendment. Asquith wrote to Lord Lytton saying that if it again passed its Second Reading, the Bill would be granted further time for debate. With the Government now seeming to pledge to end a decade of obstruction, the WSPU became increasingly confident of success.

17 June 1911
The WSPU and other suffrage organisations held a 'Coronation Procession', ending in a meeting at the Royal Albert Hall. All the women's societies participated in making the procession a success. Militants and non-militants marched, if not exactly side by side, then certainly in loyal comradeship.

In the evening, each group went to its own place, the militants going to the Royal Albert Hall, which was crowded with an enthusiastic audience. Despite the lack of firm promises from the Government, many Suffragettes believed they were on the verge of victory.

4 October 1911
Mrs Pankhurst left for another lecture tour of America. A feeling of optimism still reigned and many well-wishers came to see her off at Waterloo in a train decorated with a flag in the Suffragette colours. She announced to the crowd, *"We mean to have the vote next session. Prospects have never been so bright."*

7 November 1911
Asquith announced that a new 'Manhood Suffrage Bill', capable of amendment to include women, would be introduced in the next Parliamentary session. Suffragettes and Suffragists now feared that the Government was using the promise to expand male suffrage as a tactic to defeat the 'Conciliation Bill'.

16 November 1911
The WSPU held a mass rally at the Royal Albert Hall, and carried a resolution calling on the Government to withdraw the 'Manhood Suffrage Bill' and instead introduce a measure giving equal franchise rights to men and women. Mrs Pethick-Lawrence announced that if the Government refused to concede these just demands, she would lead a great demonstration of protest to Parliament Square on the following Tuesday. Christabel Pankhurst explained to the meeting the trick which the Government were attempting to play on women, and the necessity for standing firm at this crisis in order to prove to the Government that the WSPU refused to be betrayed.

17 November 1911
Asquith received a deputation of suffrage societies, including the WSPU. He stated that the Government would respect the wishes of the Commons if either the 'Conciliation Bill' or a 'Reform Bill' was approved by a majority. Although other less militant Suffragists argued that Asquith's pledge was genuine, the WSPU remained convinced that the Government was attempting to trick them and prepared to resume the campaign of militancy.

21 November 1911
At the Tenth Women's Parliament (held in Mrs Pankhurst's absence in America) the WSPU renewed their calls for direct action with a deputation to the House of Commons and more organised window smashing. Mass police action saw 221 women and three men arrested.

14 December 1911
Asquith told an anti-suffrage deputation that the enfranchisement of women would be 'a political mistake of a very disastrous kind' which further inflamed WSPU feelings of a Government betrayal.

The Suffragette Timeline

1912

Emmeline Pankhurst devised a shift in tactics, away from the demonstrations which had resulted in such physical injury, replacing them with attacks on property and mass actions of window smashing that women all over the country could join in relative safety. This was followed later in the year with a new tactic of vandalising post boxes and interfering with the Royal Mail. Anti-Suffrage campaigning increased, and the State began to raid suffrage organisations and use conspiracy charges against the movement's leaders. Convicted women demanded to be treated as political prisoners, and hunger-strikes became widely used as a form of protest. The emergent Labour Party began to play an increasing role in trying to win votes for women.

16 January 1912
Mrs Pankhurst returned from America.

13 February 1912
A demonstration to demand adult suffrage was organised by the Labour Party and the Fabian Society, at the Royal Albert Hall. The meeting demanded votes for everyone over age of twenty-one (not just women) and called for the Government, 'To grant to every adult, man or woman, of the right to vote for all governing bodies, both central and local.'

16 February 1912
Mrs Pankhurst announced an intensification of destructive militancy, in particular window breaking, but declared that women would only use as much force as was necessary to win. She said, *"Is not a woman's life, is not her health, are not her limbs more valuable than panes of glass?"*

23 February 1912
National Union of Women's Suffrage Societies (NUWSS) held a meeting at the Royal Albert Hall. Speakers included Mrs Henry, Millicent Fawcett, David Lloyd George MP, Mrs Philip Snowden and The Earl of Lytton.

28 February 1912
The National League for Opposing Women's Suffrage held a massive anti-Suffragette rally at the Royal Albert Hall, and passed the resolution, 'That the extension of the Parliamentary vote to women would be hostile to their own welfare and the welfare of the state, and that a change so momentous and so incalculable in its effects both socially and politically ought not to be entertained except upon a clear and deliberately expressed demand by the electorate.'

Lord Curzon stated, *"There was no class in the nation that would not suffer if votes were granted to women .... women would suffer, in the first place, because they would be taken away from that which was their proper sphere. They would have thrust upon them operations and activities for which they had neither the aptitude, the training, nor the inclination - activities which must exercise a deteriorating influence on the character, and which would draw them away from the highest and most responsible functions of womanhood."*

1 March 1912
Ignored after twice writing to Asquith requesting an interview, Mrs Pankhurst surprised the Government and the police by leading a massive window smashing rally, starting at Downing Street and followed by attacks in Piccadilly, Regent Street and Oxford Street. Many women had hidden rocks and hammers in their muffs, a popular fashion accessory at the time. Mrs Pankhurst was subsequently sentenced to two months' imprisonment.

4 March 1912
Another window smashing action began, but this time in Knightsbridge, which the police had not expected and were not prepared for. Eventually soldiers from the Knightsbridge barracks were called out to assist and 121 arrests were made. In the evening, a meeting was held at the London Pavilion followed by more window smashing. The composer Ethel Smyth smashed a window at the house of Louis Harcourt, a Cabinet Minister and one of campaign's most implacable opponents. With so many women arrested, the criminal courts were forced to sit throughout the weekend.

5 March 1912
Police raided the WSPU headquarters at Clement's Inn to arrest Mr and Mrs Pethick-Lawrence on charges of incitement.

Christabel could not be found, leading to much speculation as to her whereabouts. In fact, Christabel had fled to Paris where she continued to direct the movement with Annie Kenney's help, who travelled between London and Paris on a regular basis.

March 1912
Prison sentences for all the window smashers meant that Holloway was full, and women were sent to other prisons as far as Winson Green in Birmingham and Aylesbury. Ethel Smyth was in the cell next to Mrs Pankhurst in Holloway and when fellow composer and conductor Thomas Beecham visited, he was delighted to find her conducting her anthem 'March of the Women' to fellow Suffragettes from an upstairs window with a toothbrush!

28 March 1912
Sir Almroth Wright (a biologist of some note) wrote a letter to The Times entitled 'Suffrage Fallacies.' He attempted to medicalise militant activity by suggesting that those who persisted in it suffered from 'physiological emergencies' that lead to hysteria. The letter received considerable debate in the Press, for and against the Suffragettes, only halted by the sinking of the Titanic a few weeks later.

28 March 1912
The latest 'Conciliation Bill' came up for Second Reading in Parliament and was defeated. In the evening, record numbers of WSPU members attended an event at the Royal Albert Hall to protest. Mrs Pankhurst and Ethel Smyth were absent in Holloway Prison. The Hall had begun to question the wisdom of allowing the WSPU to use the venue, as they had to take out an Insurance Policy against future damage.

4 April 1912
Mrs Pankhurst and the Pethick-Lawrences were released on bail, to prepare to face new (more serious) charges of Conspiracy, due in Court on 15 May.

22 May 1912
The conspiracy trial ended, after seven days, with sentences of nine months for the defendants. They applied to the judge to be put in the 'First Division' category of prisoner (which was reserved for political prisoners and allowed for certain privileges such as not having to wear prison clothes), but were refused.

The harshness of the sentences caused shock around the World. They went on hunger-strike in support of this demand and were eventually granted First Division privileges, but announced they would refuse all food until the other seventy-nine Suffragette prisoners currently incarcerated were also granted equal privileges.

15 June 1912
Another WSPU meeting at the Royal Albert Hall called upon the Government to 'set at liberty the seventy-nine Suffragist prisoners, and that these prisoners of conscience shall all be placed in the First Division, and given every privilege due to them as political offenders.' The meeting also condemned the proposal of the Government 'to extend the parliamentary franchise for the benefit of men only.'
'And finally, the meeting demands that the Government shall abandon the 'Manhood Suffrage Bill' and shall in its stead introduce on Monday next a measure giving equal voting rights to men and women.'

19 June 1912
A pre-arranged hunger strike was started in Holloway. Mrs Pankhurst said, *"Holloway became a place of horror and torment."* Frederick Pethick-Lawrence joined the hunger strike from his cell in Brixton.

22 June 1912
Mrs Pankhurst was not forcibly fed and was released the following day. Mrs Pethick-Lawrence was released after being forcibly fed once, but her husband was forcibly fed for five days. Emily Wilding Davison threw herself down a prison staircase in protest.

27 June 1912
Window smashing started again but this time directed against the policy of forcible feeding. Recently released women had horrifying stories to tell of their time in jail and the Lytton family also declared that Lady Constance had developed a serious heart condition since her forcible feeding under the alias 'Jane Wharton', much to the embarrassment of the Government.

12 July 1912
From her exile in Paris, Christabel Pankhurst planned a campaign of secret arson attacks.

The Suffragette Timeline

'Votes for Women' drew a comparison between the lengthy sentences given to women for smashing a few windows in a political act, with the much more lenient sentences handed to men for assaults on girls and women.

12 July 1912
Four young women in Dublin, each received a prison sentence of six months for breaking windows in the local Post Office. Miss Houston, Miss Hasler, Miss Lloyd and Miss Webb were greeted with bouquets of flowers and cheers in the courthouse.

13 July 1912
Oxfordshire Police apprehended Helen Craggs in the grounds of Nuneham House, the country residence of Lewis Harcourt, one of the Cabinet's most outspoken politicians who believed that women should not get the vote. The policeman impounded a basket and a satchel, which together contained a bottle and two cans of inflammable oil, two boxes of matches, four tapers, nine pick-locks, twelve fire-lighters, a hammer, an electric torch, and 'a piece of American cloth smeared over with some sticky substance.'
In her bag was a note, which read, 'I myself have taken part in every peaceful method of propaganda and petition ... but I have been driven to realise that it has all been of no avail, so now I ... have done something drastic...'
Helen Craggs subsequently received nine months' imprisonment. She was, however, released after a hunger-strike of eleven days.

17 July 1912
The Government introduced yet another 'Reform Bill', but once again failed to include votes for women.

18 July 1912
While on a visit to Dublin, Prime Minister Asquith received hostile protests from Suffragettes and Suffragists. Three women were arrested for trying to burn down the Theatre Royal in Dublin and while travelling to his hotel, a hatchet was thrown into his carriage. The three women received very harsh sentences. They were denied political rights and went on hunger-strike. Two of the women were force fed and the other was released in a very serious condition. To protest the harsh sentences, the WSPU organised a rally to be held in Phoenix Park, Dublin on 8 September 1912.

October 1912
Long-term Pankhurst supporters the Pethick-Lawrences, unhappy about the increasingly militant tactics of the WSPU, were asked to leave the Union by Christabel and Mrs Pankhurst. They retained ownership of the paper 'Votes for Women' but severed ties with the WSPU. In response, the Union launched its own magazine, 'The Suffragette', edited by Christabel.

17 October 1912
In a meeting at the Royal Albert Hall, Mrs Pankhurst announced the split with the Pethick-Lawrences and went on to direct her followers to intensify the militant campaign. She was quoted, *"There is something that Government's care more for than human life, and that is the security of property...I incite this meeting to rebellion."*

4 November 1912
The first reports of the new Suffragette campaign tactic of attacking The Royal Mail began to emerge. A corrosive liquid had been poured into a post-box near Piccadilly Circus. This was to become a common method of showing anger with the Government, and many post-boxes were damaged up and down the country. This came the day after yet another attempt to expand the franchise to women had been opposed by the Government and defeated in the House of Commons.

5 November 1912
The Royal Albert Hall was crowded again for the demonstration, organised by the NUWSS, to demand the inclusion of women in the latest 'Reform Bill'. Mrs Henry Fawcett presided, and the resolution was moved by Lord Robert Cecil, and seconded by Mr W C Anderson, chairman of the Independent Labour Party.

The Times reported:
'The announcement by the chairman that Mr Snowden's amendment to enfranchise women under Home Rule had been defeated was received with loud cries of 'shame'. Lord Robert Cecil said he had come from the House of Commons. 'Shame'. Even so, the first thing he had to do was congratulate the meeting on the steady, and continuous advance of the cause of women's suffrage. (Cheers). Despite the opinion of Lord Curzon, he was profoundly convinced that women had much that they could bring to the state.'

14 November 1912
The radical Labour MP George Lansbury resigned his Parliamentary seat in Bromley and Bow in the East End of London thereby forcing a by-election. Lansbury had been frustrated at the lack of progress on women's suffrage in Parliament and took this brave decision to bring this issue to the fore. Standing again as the 'Women's Suffrage and Socialist' candidate, Lansbury drew support from both the militant Suffragettes, and Millicent Fawcett and the law-abiding Suffragists. The whole of the Bow Road area was full of organisations campaigning for Lansbury, although there was also an Anti-Suffragette shop with a sign for a 'No Petticoat Government.'

26 November 1912
Lansbury narrowly lost his seat by 751 votes to the Conservative and anti-Suffrage candidate and later questioned the wisdom of his decision. However, a decade later, Lansbury was finally re-elected as an MP in 1922 and went on to become leader of the Labour Party 1932-1935.

28 November 1912
A five-day attack on pillar boxes began using various liquids including ink, tar, paint and sometimes corrosive and explosive substances. Although this became a subject for many comical cartoons in the Press, it lost the Suffragettes support from the general public.

19 December 1912
Three Suffragettes were arrested for damaging the contents of letterboxes in Deptford, Lewisham and Putney, using ink, tar and paint. This method of protesting did mean that women could protest without the risk of male violence, however police were known to sometimes lurk near post-boxes hoping to catch a Suffragette in the act.

The Suffragette Timeline

1913

Militancy reached its peak, with the Suffragettes moving on from random acts of window smashing, to an even more destructive form of terrorism (arson and bombs) as they attacked Establishment targets designed to bring maximum publicity. Faced with massive public condemnation of the brutality of force feeding hunger-strikers, the Government introduced the notoriously anti-liberal 'Cat and Mouse Act', which enabled them to drag the Suffragette leadership in and out of prison, almost at will. In June, Emily Wilding Davison became the first nationally recognised Suffragette martyr.

9 January 1913
May Billinghurst and Louisa Gay were sentenced, at the Old Bailey, to eight months for damage to the Royal Mail but were placed in the more lenient First Division in prison as the Recorder 'recognised the purity of their motives.' Nevertheless, the indomitable May Billinghurst, confined to a wheelchair, still declared that she would go on hunger-strike.

13 January 1913
A few days before the debate on the women's suffrage amendments to the Government 'Reform Bill' (scheduled for 17 January), Mrs Pankhurst called for another truce in the campaign of militancy.

23 January 1913
A deputation of working women from all over the UK came to give evidence at Parliament and to ask for the vote. Twenty women from a group of three hundred were chosen to meet Lloyd George and Sir Edward Grey.

One of the women, Mrs King, a fisher-woman from Newhaven in Edinburgh told the enquiry:
"I have travelled 400 miles on behalf of hundreds of fisher-women. Sometimes the woman has to work much harder than the man, because when the man's work is done he goes to bed, but we have to go out and sell fish. We have to get up at 5 o'clock in the morning, and sometimes we are not home until 6 o'clock at night. Then we have our household duties and sometimes it is 12 o'clock before we go to bed...Gentlemen, you have made a promise and see that you keep it and grant us the vote, and I will take it home to Scotland!"

Lloyd George insisted that Asquith's pledge to provide time for the women's suffrage amendments to the Bill would be kept. He agreed to meet the deputation again for further consultation after the debate.

January 1913
The debate on the women's suffrage amendments to the 'Reform Bill' ended when Asquith accepted The Speaker's ruling that the Bill could not proceed. He agreed that time could be granted in the coming session for the passage of a Private Member's Bill. All the suffrage societies angrily rejected to this offer and the WSPU declared an immediate renewal of militancy. Mrs Pankhurst criticised Asquith stating, *"Whether he had done the thing deliberately, with the plain intention of selling out the women, or whether ignorance of parliamentary rules accounted for the failure of the bill was immaterial."*

27 January 1913
Asquith announced the withdrawal of the 'Reform Bill'. In response, the WSPU truce ended in an outbreak of unprecedented militancy. Telephone wires were cut, works of art destroyed, boat houses and sports pavilions burned and golf courses vandalised with slogans burned into the grass with acid. Mrs Pankhurst later stated of this period, *"Now we indeed lighted the torch, and we did it with the absolute conviction that no other course was open to us."*

28 January 1913
Flora Drummond tried to lead another group of twenty working women to see Lloyd George (as he had promised at the meeting five days before) but this time he refused to meet with them. The women marched to Parliament where the group was met with great police brutality. As soon as news of the failure of the deputation spread, windows were smashed and thirty arrests are made.

28 January 1913
Mrs Cousins, Mrs Connery and Mrs Hoskins were arrested for breaking fifteen windows in the upper yard of Dublin Castle. Mrs Cousins was carrying an umbrella with a lump of lead attached when she was arrested. She said that what they had done was a protest against the treachery of the Government and Leader of the Irish Parliamentary Party Mr John Redmond. The women were each sentenced to one month hard labour.

29 January 1913
Flora Drummond appeared in court facing charges of willful damage and destruction. Eye witness accounts agreed that, the day before, she was treated with such brutality that she had fallen unconscious, and as she said in court, *"It would take a great deal to make me faint."*

30 January 1913
Flora Drummond was released from Holloway after only 24 hours in jail. She was told by the Governor of the prison that a gentleman had paid the fine and she was free to go. On her release, she again wrote to Lloyd George and asked if she could bring her deputation of 'Working Women' back to meet him, but unsurprisingly, he again refused.

30 January 1913
Asquith travelled to Scotland to receive the freedom of the City of Dundee, but the Suffragettes were one step ahead and disrupted every meeting he attended. The Daily Express headlined the next day with 'The Hunted Premier' and described how a Miss Mary Grant, daughter of a local minister had shouted, *"How dare you come to Dundee, you traitor to women!"*

Going further, a member of the Dundee branch of the Women's Freedom League declared, *"We object most emphatically to any honour bestowed on a man who absolutely refuses to confer justice on women, and considering that Dundee is a woman's city, and it's trade is produced by women's labours, we think it is an insult that such a man should dare show face here, and accept freedom from those to whom he denies it."*

3 February 1913
A working-class woman, Mrs Leonora Cohen from Leeds, was charged with damaging the jewel house at the Tower of London. She had been in Flora Drummond's deputation of women only days earlier. Her case was dismissed on a technicality, but now many tourist attractions discussed shutting their doors to the public.

8 February 1913
The Orchid House at Kew Gardens was attacked by Suffragettes, with windows smashed and precious plants dug up.

10 February 1913
Four women were arrested after Establishment clubs were attacked in Pall Mall (the Carlton, the Junior Carlton, the Reform Club, the Oxford and Cambridge, Schomberg house and the residence of Prince Christian) with stones, pieces of lead, iron nuts and clay balls.

10 February 1913
Mrs Pankhurst spoke at a meeting at the London Pavilion with a bunch of orchids in front of her, as she took personal responsibility and justified the violence at Kew and elsewhere.

19 February 1913
The Suffragette bomb
In the early hours, a house under construction in Surrey for Lloyd George, Chancellor of the Exchequer, was destroyed by a bomb set by Suffragettes.
Meanwhile, Christabel Pankhurst, in exile in Paris, declared:
"..if men use explosives and bombs for their own purpose they call it war, and the throwing of a bomb that destroys other people is then described as a glorious and heroic deed. Why should women not make use of the same weapons as men. It is not only war we have declared. We are fighting for a revolution."

20 February 1913
The Tea Pavilion at Kew Gardens was burned down by Lillian Lenton and Olive Wharry. Cards were found at the site which said 'Peace on Earth and goodwill to men - when women get the vote.' They were later sentenced to eighteen months in prison. While in court, Wharry also stated that morally she was not guilty, and would not submit to punishment. Once behind bars, the pair immediately went on hunger-strike and Wharry's prison scrapbook (held at the British Library) revealed that she went thirty-two days without eating before being released. Lillian Lenton was released, after she contracted pleurisy from the forcible feeding.

20 February 1913
The Pavilion of the Old Manchester Golf Club was set on fire, and corrosive liquid used on the greens at Horsforth Golf Links near Leeds.

24 February 1913
In a meeting in Cardiff, Mrs Pankhurst accepted responsibility for the militant acts and declared, *"We have blown up Lloyd George's house!"*

The Suffragette Timeline

25 February 1913
Mrs Pankhurst was arrested 'for procuring and inciting persons to commit offences contrary to the Malicious Injuries to Property Act 1881.' The case was scheduled to be heard in 1 April at London's Central Criminal Court.

1 March 1913
Two-hundred protestors marched twelve miles from Bow Road to Holloway Prison, to give three cheers outside the prison for Sylvia Pankhurst and Miss Lansbury.

10 March 1913
Five brave women tried to present a petition to King George V on his way to Parliament to deliver the King's speech which, yet again, made no mention of votes for women. Each of the women held a copy of a petition calling for the vote and stating that 'Votes for women is the only cure for militancy.' The petitions were tied in Suffragette ribbons of green, purple and white but as they tried to approach the King's carriage in the Mall, they were quickly arrested. In court, all five women pleaded their innocence under the Bill of Rights, by which a subject cannot be arrested for petitioning the King. But this was disregarded in court and the defendants were sentenced to between three weeks and a month in prison even though they had not even got within a few feet of the King.

18 March 1913
A meeting was held in Kingsway Hall in London to protest against the forcible feeding of Suffragettes. George Bernard Shaw, one of the few notable men to speak out about the barbaric treatment of the Suffragettes, said, *"If you take a woman and torture her you torture me. If you take Mrs Pankhurst's daughter and torture her you are torturing my daughter. If you take Miss Pankhurst's mother and torture her you are torturing my mother. I go further and say that if you torturing my mother you are torturing me. I tell you these are denials of fundamental rights are really a violation of the soul."*

25 March 1913
The 'Cat And Mouse Act' passed
In the meantime, the Government rushed through 'The Prisoners Temporary Discharge for Ill-Health Act' which became known as the notorious 'Cat and Mouse Act'.

Under this law, hunger strikers, if certified to be unfit to remain in prison by a doctor, could be released on license to recover their health, and then be rearrested when they were well enough to continue their sentences. The power to forcibly feed prisoners was retained.
(see the article in Suffragette Stories)

March 1913
The Royal Albert Hall, home to many of the most important meetings in the suffrage campaign, received a letter questioning the advisability of letting it out to Suffragettes in the future, and subsequently discussed a possible ban at their next Council meeting.

1 April 1913
Mrs Pankhurst was tried for incitement to commit a felony and sentenced to three years' penal servitude (usually hard labour). In fact, she only served six weeks of her sentence and was released on special license after nine days on hunger-strike. The pattern of her hunger (and later thirst) strikes and release on license was to be repeated several times over the coming months.

8 April 1913
After she publicly defended the policy of property attacks, Annie Kenney was arrested and charged with incitement. After several adjournments of her case, she was discharged (with Flora Drummond) to face more serious charges. Her place as the WSPU's main organiser was taken by Grace Roe.

10 April 1913
George Lansbury MP and Flora Drummond addressed a huge audience of Suffragettes at the Royal Albert Hall. Lansbury made an impassioned speech in support of the militant women:-

"Why are we here and why are these brave women carrying on this crusade? Because they believe in something much bigger than the vote; they believe in human freedom. That is what they are out for. (Cheers). The other day I had sent to me by a young girl from the East End one of the most pathetic letters I have ever seen. She told a story of how she worked at a confectionery factory, making sweets and jam, to the tune of something like six shillings a week. She, had no one to help her live, and was driven to make the balance by other means.

"Those men here, if there are any, who are crying out against what the women are doing, what are you doing? You go out of this hall and you see the girls on the streets. You read of sweated wages, but you do not really know why one of the Suffragist prisoners said, when brought up before a magistrate, If you lived where I live and saw the misery I see, instead of breaking one window you would break a hundred!'"

Both speakers were arrested after the event for inciting people to commit a breach of the peace.

15 April 1913
The Home Office banned WSPU open-air meetings. In retaliation, the house of Arthur Du Gros, (anti-suffrage MP for St. Leonards) was gutted by a fire set by Suffragettes.

18 April 1913
Two enterprising Suffragettes 'captured' the Monument in the City of London for several hours. Equipped with heavy iron bars, the Suffragette flag and a large banner inscribed 'Death or Victory', they managed to barricade themselves in the gallery of the top of the tower. They showered the crowds below with leaflets demanding women's suffrage until the police eventually took back control. Gertrude Shaw and Ethel Spark, were released without charge. Not only had their protest successfully caused the desired disruption and achieved maximum publicity for the campaign it also, according to the 'Votes for Women' newspaper, added one more success 'to the lists of triumphs of female ingenuity'.

30 April 1913
The police raided WSPU headquarters and arrested more Union personnel, seized copy prepared for 'The Suffragette', and two days later, arrested the manager of the printing company. Grace Roe escaped to Paris to confer with Christabel.

2 May 1913
Annie Kenney, Flora Drummond and the staff arrested in the raid three days earlier were put on trial for 'conspiracy to commit malicious damage.'

5 May 1913
The Private Members' Bill which Asquith had suggested on 18 January 1913 (to buy-off Suffragette opposition as an alternative to the 'Reform Bill') was defeated.

25 May 1913
'Women's May Day' was held in East London. The women of Bow, Bromley, Poplar, and neighbouring districts had prepared for it for many weeks, making hundreds of almond branches, which were carried in a great procession with purple, white and green flags, and caps of Liberty flying above them from the East India Dock gates to Victoria Park. A vast crowd of people, the biggest ever seen in East London, assembled to hear the speakers from twenty platforms.

26 May 1913
Mrs Pankhurst was re-arrested under the 'Cat And Mouse Act' as she left Ethel Smyth's house in the country. She started a five-day hunger-strike before being released again. After many trips to prison and hunger-strikes, fears began to grow about her health.

3 June 1913
The WSPU organised a fund-raising summer fair at the Empress Rooms. It was attended by Emily Wilding Davison who told a friend that she would be at the Epsom Derby the next day and to look in the papers for something she planned to do.

4 June 1913
The most famous Suffragette protest
As the Epsom Derby got under way, Emily Wilding Davison ran on to the track and attempted to grab the bridle of Anmer, the horse owned by King George V, to attach a Votes For Women sash. The horse collided with her and as she fell to the ground, she was trampled by its hooves, and crushed as it then fell on top of her. Emily had previously been one of the Suffragettes' most militant activists, having been arrested nine times and frequently on hunger-strike.

5 June 1913
Civil actions for damages (by over ninety firms), were taken against Mrs Pankhurst, Mr and Mrs Pethick-Lawrence, and others, in connection with window breaking between November 1911 and March 1912. The claims were eventually upheld.

8 June 1913
The Suffragette Martyr
Emily Wilding Davison died of her injuries, four days after being trampled at the Epsom Derby.

The Suffragette Timeline

10 June 1913
The Royal Albert Hall Council took the decision to ban meetings of the WSPU.

14 June 1913
Emily Wilding Davison's funeral, organised by the WSPU, saw thousands of Suffragettes accompany the coffin, with tens of thousands of people lining the streets of London. Mrs Pankhurst was arrested on her way to the funeral and her empty carriage followed the coffin. After a service in Bloomsbury, the coffin was taken by train to the family grave in Morpeth, Northumberland. She was laid to rest in the churchyard of St. Mary the Virgin, in a family plot where her father was buried in 1893. Her gravestone bore the WSPU slogan 'Deeds Not Words'.

17 June 1913
The conspiracy trial of Annie Kenney and others ended, with sentences ranging from twelve to eighteen months handed out while Mrs Winston Churchill and Miss Violet Asquith rather ghoulishly looked on. The convicted prisoners embarked on a cycle of hunger-strikes followed by release and re-arrest under the 'Cat and Mouse Act'.

18 June 1913
The 'Women's Pilgrimage' organised by Millicent Fawcett's National Union of Women's Suffrage Societies, began from places all around the country to march to London along eight main routes.

26 July 1913
The 'Pilgrimage' came to an end in Hyde Park, London. The Suffragists who had marched from all corners of the UK, had encountered support but also some violence along the way. The group which had started from Land's End had a good reception in Exeter, but were then pelted with rotten eggs and cabbages in Cheltenham. The Times reported: 'On Saturday the pilgrimage of the law abiding advocates of votes for women ended in a great gathering in Hyde Park attended by some 50,000 persons. The proceedings were quite orderly and devoid of any untoward incident. The proceedings, indeed, were as much a demonstration against militancy as one in favour of women's suffrage.'

9 August 1913
Thousands of doctors gathered at the Royal Albert Hall for the International Medical Congress. But while the men talked inside, Suffragettes demonstrated outside to highlight the brutality of forcible feeding, wearing sandwich-boards which read 'The English Government is murdering women.' Many doctors, even those opposed to votes for women, agreed that the policy was terribly dangerous and inhumane.

July to December 1913
Mrs Pankhurst, WSPU leaders, and rank-and-file Suffragettes were repeatedly dragged in and out of prison under the 'Cat and Mouse Act'. Mrs Pankhurst devised a new tactic of the thirst and sleep strike, and spent several weeks on the run. In August she and Annie Kenney escaped to join Christabel in Paris. Meanwhile, the militancy continued. Mansions were destroyed, pillar boxes attacked, tennis courts and golf courses damaged with acid, dummy bombs left on the underground and in public buildings, real bombs manufactured and used in arson attacks, and church services interrupted. One estimate put the value of damage by arson in 1913 at £510,150. The Suffragettes continued to make sure that no people were hurt during their attacks on property.

18 October 1913
Mrs Pankhurst arrived on a fund-raising tour in America, only to find she was to be deported. After two days on Ellis Island, she was finally admitted on the orders of the President.

1 November 1913
A large demonstration on behalf of the Dublin Strikers was held at the Royal Albert Hall. Sylvia Pankhurst spoke on the platform, alongside left-wing Independent Labour Party (ILP) representatives George Lansbury and James Connolly. As a consequence of Sylvia's appearance at this meeting, she was summoned to the WSPU headquarters in exile in Paris and told by Christabel that the East London Federation must become a separate organisation at once.

4 December 1913
Mrs Pankhurst was rearrested at sea on her return journey to England. She was remanded to Exeter prison, where she was released after a four-day hunger-strike.

The Suffragette Timeline

December 1913
A performance of the opera Jeanne d'Arc by Raymond Roze attended by King George and Queen Mary was disrupted by Suffragettes, as three women hung a banner stating, 'King George, women are being tortured in your Majesty's prisons.'

16 December 1913
Bottles of corrosive acid were found in pillar-boxes in Dublin. Large numbers of letters were destroyed.

18 December 1913
Two bombs exploded at Holloway Prison in North London where many Suffragettes were being held. Although no one was arrested, Suffragettes were suspected of the crime as long pieces of fuse ran from the site of the explosions to the back garden of a house rented by campaigners. At the house, police found a piece of ribbon and a long hair. The bomb was intended to scare the prison officials rather than harm anyone, although several nearby houses lost windows in the explosion.

19 December 1913
A large coach and motor builders warehouse at Sutton was firebombed, with damage estimated at £1,000. Despite the lack of evidence, Suffragettes were suspected.

20 December 1913
A large unoccupied house at Lansdown, Bath, valued at £2,500 was ruined by fire. Suffrage literature was found nearby.

21 December 1913
Alstone Manor, an unoccupied house near Cheltenham was partially burned down. The Beryl, an 800 ton steam yacht owned by Lord Inverclyde, was destroyed by fire while lying off Rosneath Pier, Gareloch. Suffragettes were suspected of these attacks, although no evidence was found.

29 December 1913
Suffragette and Indian royalty, Princess Sophia Duleep Singh, was charged in a London court with refusing to pay her taxes. She declared that until women obtained the vote she would refuse to pay them: *"If I am not a fit person for the purpose of representation, why should I be a fit person for taxation? Taxation without representation is tyranny."*

December 1913
The East London Suffragettes organised a 'Suffrage School', which included a series of educational lectures and entertainment from the Actresses Franchise League. Tickets were available from Miss Jenkins, at 321 Roman Road which was the headquarters of the East London Federation (ELF) and included talks on 'History of the Suffragette Movement', 'The Legal Position of the British Wife and Mother' and a lecture about the 'Effects of Forcible Feeding on Suffragette Prisoners.' This last lecture was delivered by Dr. Flora Murray, a Scottish doctor who was also an active Suffragette. During the First World War, she established (with her friend and colleague Dr. Louisa Garrett Anderson) the Endell Street Military Hospital, in Covent Garden, London which was staffed entirely by women. Their motto was 'Deeds Not Words.'

The Suffragette Timeline

1914

Militant Suffragette action continued, until Mrs Pankhurst decided to suspend it in support of the Government, after war was declared on Germany in August. In response, the Government released all suffrage campaigners from prison.

January 1914
Due to the intransigence of Government ministers, Mrs Pankhurst decided to petition the King directly and wrote to him requesting an audience. The request is refused.

4 February 1914
Suffragettes set fire to Aberuchill Castle in Scotland.

7 February 1914
Sylvia Pankhurst, who had been campaigning independently in the East End of London, was asked by her mother and sister to leave the WSPU because of her increasing involvement in socialist politics. She travelled to France to meet her sister in exile, whereupon Christabel issued a statement declaring that Sylvia's campaign group in the East End was to separate from the WSPU.

8 February 1914
Mrs Pankhurst, who spent January with Christabel in Paris, returned to England and announced her intention to make a speech from the balcony of 2 Campden Hill Square (nicknamed 'Mouse Castle' as a refuge for Suffragettes on their release from prison) where she was staying. A woman bodyguard armed with clubs was there to protect her, and an attempt to arrest her failed. A few days later she made a similar speech from another location, and again managed to evade arrest.

14 Feb 1914
Millicent Fawcett presided at the Royal Albert Hall at a public meeting organized by the National Union of Women's Suffrage Societies. The Hall was filled, and on the platform were several hundred delegates from labour organizations. Mrs Fawcett said the meeting was unprecedented in the history of the movement, in that it demonstrated the support and sympathy of men's organizations.

Supporters at the meeting included professionals and businessmen, and many hundreds of delegates from town councils, trade councils, and trade unions. It was hoped that politicians would listen to the demands of those already enfranchised, having 'neglected the cry of the vote-less'. But yet again, Mr Asquith refused to receive a deputation from the meeting.

9 March 1914
After several weeks on the run, Mrs Pankhurst was at last arrested at St Andrew's Hall in Glasgow, and despite the attempts of her bodyguard to protect her, she was violently removed by the police.

10 March 1914
Mary Richardson slashed the famous painting 'Rokeby Venus' by Velázquez at the National Gallery with an axe that she managed hide under her dress. When asked why, she said, *"I have tried to destroy the picture of the most beautiful woman in mythological history as a protest against the Government for destroying Mrs Pankhurst, who is the most beautiful character in modern history."*

At that time Mrs Pankhurst was on hunger-strike in Holloway and there were serious concerns about her health. The slashing of the picture caused a backlash in Britain against Suffragette militancy and led to many art galleries and museums refusing to allow in unaccompanied women.

Mary Richardson, one of the most militant Suffragettes, was with Emily Wilding Davison when she stepped out in front of the King's horse at the Epsom Derby, and also committed a number of acts of arson, smashed windows at the Home Office and bombed a railway station. She was arrested nine times, and was forcibly fed in Holloway.

14 March 1914
Mrs Pankhurst was released after yet another hunger-strike, still recovering from bruises received during her arrest in Glasgow.

22 March 1914
Sylvia Pankhurst led a procession of women from Bow, in the East End of London to Westminster Abbey. The procession was 800 mainly working class men and women. Sylvia was carried in a special stretcher as her health had been seriously damaged by the months of forced feeding in prison.

When the peaceful procession arrived at the Abbey, the doors were locked even though the bells rang out for Evensong. The crowd outside sang 'Onward Christian Soldiers' and listened to some words from Sylvia although her voice was painfully weak. She reminded the crowd that it was Mothering Sunday and said, *"We have come here to ask one higher than the Government that the women of this country, the mothers of this country, shall have the power to make or mark a Government in order that they may get better conditions for themselves."*

4 April 1914
The Ulster Unionist militants organised a demonstration in Hyde Park. To protest against the refusal to allow the WSPU to hold meetings there, members marched to the Park and interrupted Ulster speakers, as police struggled to suppress them. Mrs Drummond was arrested and tried for obstruction, but refused to cooperate with the court and later talked constantly throughout her trial.

April 1914
Kitty Marion was released from Holloway in a severely malnourished state from being forcibly fed 232 times.

16 April 1914
A large unoccupied house in Londonderry set was on fire, with suffragist message found at the scene.

17 April 1914
Yarmouth Pier Pavilion was destroyed by bomb, with damage estimated at £15,000-£20,000. Attempts were made to burn down Kempton Park grandstand, and the Empire Music Hall in Kingston was damaged by fire.

18 April 1914
The Tea house at Belle Vue, Belfast was destroyed by fire. Separately, pillar-boxes were attacked in Lewisham and Catford.

20 April 1914
Questions were asked in the House of Commons about the level of damage done by the militant Suffragette action and what steps the Government were taking to protect public and private property.

22 April 1914
Annandale Hall in Belfast was damaged by fire.

5 and 6 May 1914
A Private Member's Bill brought by Lord Selborne in the House of Lords, which would have enfranchised women municipal voters, was defeated.

21 May 1914
Mrs Pankhurst led the last great WSPU militant deputation, trying to gain an audience with the King. Thousands of police were brought in to repel the hundreds of women who had travelled from all over the country, and the ensuing violence even exceeded that of 'Black Friday'. Sixty-six women and two men were arrested. Mrs Pankhurst was amongst those arrested and again she promptly went on hunger and thirst-strike. Also that morning, police raided a flat where WSPU organiser Nellie Hall was staying with her mother and sister. They discovered gunpowder, fuses, flints, fuses and hammers, and arrested the women.

22 May 1914
Militant Suffragette actions occurred all over the country in protest at the arrest of Mrs Pankhurst and the awful violence used on hundreds of other women the day before. Pictures were slashed at the National Gallery, a mummy case broken at the British Museum, a portrait of the King in the Royal Scottish Academy was damaged, and a bomb was placed outside a church in Edinburgh. At a matinee at His Majesty's Theatre, Christabel Pankhurst announced that The King was now to be treated like any other anti-suffrage Cabinet Minister, accusing him of being like a 'Russian Tsar.' At the same time, Suffragettes chained themselves to the railings outside Buckingham Palace.

23 May 1914
Police raided WSPU headquarters and arrested General Secretary Grace Roe, and charged her with conspiring with Nellie Hall. Nellie's mother and sister were released, but she and Grace Roe were put on trial. They refused to cooperate with the court, and were refused bail. While on remand, they were forcibly fed for seven weeks before their case was heard, and both women were sentenced to three months' imprisonment.

24 May 1914
Sylvia Pankhurst led the East London Federation of Suffragettes to the May Day Procession in Victoria Park in London's East End. Her bodyguard of twenty-five women had taken the precaution of chaining themselves together.

However, a running battle between the police and Sylvia's supporters ensued but the police managed to smash the chains with truncheons and Sylvia was re-arrested.

26 May 1914
Mrs Pankhurst was released again from Holloway.

27 May 1914
Two panes of glass smashed were smashed at Buckingham Palace

28 May 1914
Three windows were damaged at the National Gallery. Separately, a bomb was found on a goods train at Wellingborough.

3 June 1914
Holloway prison surgeon, Doctor Forward, and two police constables were horse-whipped in the street outside the prison. In a day of militant action, a house in Belfast was set ablaze and two pictures were seriously damaged in the Dore Gallery in London.

4 June 1914
Mary Blomfield, a Suffragette sympathiser was being presented at Court with her sister. When she met King George V, she dropped to her knees and declared *"For God's sake stop forcible feeding."* The two women were removed from the Royal party and taken away by their horrified mother for a long holiday out of the country! Subsequently, Royal garden parties in London and Windsor were cancelled for the rest of the season.

10 June 1914
The British-American Peace Centenary Ball at the Royal Albert Hall was disturbed by a militant Suffragette.

11 June 1914
The hunger-strike of the Suffragettes was debated in the Commons. Summing up the methods of overcoming militancy Home Secretary McKenna said, *"The first is to let them die. That is, I should say, at the present moment, the most popular."* Other methods raised in the debate included deportation, treating them as lunatics, and even actually giving them the vote.

McKenna concluded that none of these methods would be adopted, but that he would consider taking civil and criminal action against WSPU subscribers, and he asked the newspapers to stop reporting the militant acts.

20 June 1914
A deputation of working women organised by Sylvia Pankhurst was received by Asquith who said (rather surprisingly) he agreed with them, and that if women were to have the vote it should be on the same terms as men.

8 July 1914
Mrs Pankhurst attempted to go back to work but was re-arrested immediately. In Holloway once again she began a hunger-strike but this time was released after three days, in a very weak and unwell condition.

16 July 1914
Mrs Pankhurst attempted to address another meeting in Holland Park Hall. But once again she was re-arrested, but lying on a stretcher and clearly in poor health, was released after the meeting.

31 July 1914
An explosion was heard late at night at Lisburn Cathedral, Northern Ireland. The explosion, which blew out one of the oldest stained glass windows, was planned by four local Suffragettes led by Lillian Metge, who had to receive police protection when arrested. All the windows of her house were smashed by residents opposed to her actions and the Government threatened to raise the rates to pay for the damage caused. Ultimately, no charges were pressed against the four women due to the start of the Great War, as they were released by order of the Home Secretary.

4 August 1914
The First World War began
Britain declared war on Germany, and the militant Suffragette campaign came to a sudden halt.
Emmeline Pankhurst and the WSPU threw their weight behind the war effort and in return, an amnesty was granted to all Suffragette prisoners.

10 August 1914
Mrs Pankhurst asked: *"What is the use of fighting for a vote if we have not got a country to vote in?"* However, not all Suffragettes and Suffragists felt the same way and many, including Sylvia Pankhurst did not support the war, and argued that it was the male-dominated, unbalanced nature of politics that had led the World to the war in the first place.

10 August 1914
All Suffragette prisoners were released from prison, and Mrs Pankhurst formally suspended WSPU activities. The non-militant NUWSS dropped all suffrage campaigning and turned itself into a Women's Active Service Corps, while a breakaway group formed the Women's International League. The United Suffragists (formed earlier in 1914 to unite militant and non-militant suffragists) did continue with suffrage work and produced an edition of 'Votes for Women' (which Mr and Mrs Pethick-Lawrence had donated to them). The Women's Freedom League continued suffrage work.

8 September 1914
Christabel returned to England to speak at the London Opera House on the subject of 'The German Peril'. Mrs Pankhurst toured the country in support of the war effort, making a number of recruitment speeches.

The Suffragette Timeline

1915 - 1917

The women's movement swung behind the war effort. Securing the vote for men in the trenches became a more important issue for many reformers in Parliament. Women became increasingly important to the war effort.

24 January 1915
A demonstration took place in Trafalgar Square to 'protest at women being exploited to protect men.'

March 1915
The 'Shell Scandal', in which a shortage of munitions led to the failure of a British army offensive, caused the fall of the Liberal Government. As a result, it became clear that the war effort required the recruitment of more women to work in factories.

16 April 1915
'The Suffragette' magazine reappeared after a short break.

13 March 1915
At a conference of women's organisations called by the Board of Trade to encourage women to register for war work, many suffrage societies demanded this be linked to equal pay and the vote. However, the NUWSS and Women's Liberal and Conservative Associations promised unconditional cooperation to the Government. The WSPU did not attend.

17 July 1915
The WSPU, now calling itself the Women's Party, called for compulsory national service for war work by women and organised a procession of 30,000 women in support of the demand which was paid for by Lloyd George from Government funds. They marched under the slogan 'We demand the right to serve' and more factories and businesses began to hire women.

15 October 1915
'The Suffragette' magazine was re-born as 'Britannia', a patriotic, pro-war publication.

5 November 1915
As the demand for the enfranchisement of the men on war service grew, the Government responded by delaying the General Election for eight months. On 5 November a Private Member's 'Service Franchise Bill' was introduced, but the Government said it would deal with the matter itself. Amidst rumours that a 'Franchise Bill' was to be introduced, those suffrage societies that were still active wrote to Asquith to remind him of the women's claims.

18 November 1915
The WSPU's 'Great Patriotic Meeting' at the Royal Albert Hall was cancelled because the management of the Hall had seen a leaflet criticizing the Government.

January 1916
A conference of suffrage societies called by Sylvia Pankhurst was unable to reach agreement on a programme of how exactly to campaign for adult suffrage.

March 1916
A Consultative Committee of Constitutional Women's Suffrage Societies was formed in response to the Government's proposed changes to the electoral register.

April 1916
The Liberal and Unionist War Committees demanded a vote for all soldiers in the trenches. Sylvia Pankhurst called another conference of suffrage organisations, which was held two months later in June.

2 September 1916
A National Council for Adult Suffrage was established at a second conference of suffrage organisations.

14 August 1916
After years of obstruction, Asquith was finally converted to the cause of women's suffrage. He was persuaded, he announced, by the argument that if 'a new class of electors, on whatever ground of State Service is formed, then women who have rendered as effective service in the prosecution of the War as any class of the community' also had a claim.

The Suffragette Timeline

1 October 1916
At a meeting in Queen's Hall, Mrs Pankhurst repudiated Asquith's statement and suggested he was using women to prevent soldiers from being enfranchised. She and Christabel demand votes for soldiers, and votes for women.

12 October 1916
A Speaker's Conference was established to report on electoral reform.

7 December 1916
The 'Franchise Reform Bill' passed its Third Reading, having decided to settle the age limit for women voters at thirty, not thirty-five.

January 1917
The Speaker's Conference reported and recommended the granting of the vote to women over thirty who are local government electors or wives of local government electors, and university graduates over thirty . There was no property qualification for men, who could all vote from the age of twenty-one. Despite the obvious inequality towards women, many suffrage organisations, including the NUWSS, accepted these terms.

19 June 1917
The 'Representation of the People's Act' was passed by the House of Commons with a majority of 385 to 55. Lord Curzon, President of The National League for Opposing Women's Suffrage dropped his opposition to avoid a clash between The Commons and The House of Lords.

23 August 1917
The grille in the Ladies Gallery at the Houses of Parliament was finally removed.

The Suffragette Timeline

1918-1928

Victory was achieved, but not finally until 1928. Historians would debate for decades whether the Suffragettes actually won their campaign, or if the granting of votes for women was an inevitable consequence of the end of the First World War.

January 1918
In a last-ditch attempt to stop progress, Mrs Humphry Ward led an anti-suffragist deputation to the House of Lords arguing that the women's suffrage should not be introduced without a referendum. Nevertheless, the Act passed in the upper chamber.

6 February 1918
The 'Representation of the People Act' finally received Royal Ascent and became law. It granted the Parliamentary vote all men over twenty-one and to women over thirty (who were occupiers, or wives of occupiers of land or premises of not less than £5 annual value), and to women over thirty who were university graduates.

16 March 1918
The WSPU held a 'Patriotic Meeting and Celebration of the Woman's Suffrage Victory' at the Royal Albert Hall. Speakers included Emmeline Pankhurst, Christabel Pankhurst, Flora Drummond, and Annie Kenney.

14 December 1918
Women vote for Parliament for the first time
The first General Election after the war was held. Known as the 'Khaki Election' due to the large number of returning soldiers, women were allowed to vote for Parliament for the first time. Under 'The Parliament (Qualification of Women) Act', women could also now stand for Parliament. Seventeen women did so, including Christabel Pankhurst, who was unsuccessful. The first woman to be elected was Constance Markievicz, but as a member of Sinn Fein, she had disqualified herself by refusing to take the oath.

1 December 1919
Nancy Astor became the first woman to take her seat in the House of Commons. However, her election was not greeted enthusiastically by everyone as she had not taken part in the Suffrage campaign and was American, but she did prove to be an excellent campaigner for many women's issues and was not intimidated by the all-male House of Commons. She once quipped that after marrying the hugely rich Waldorf Astor, *"I married beneath me, all women do."*
(See the article in Suffragette Stories)

23 December 1919
Under 'The Sex Disqualification (Removal) Act' women were no longer barred from civil or judicial offices (including judge, barrister and solicitor), from any profession, or from membership of any incorporated society.

14 June 1928
Emmeline Pankhurst died, at the age of 69, in a Wimpole Street nursing home.

18 June 1928
Mrs Pankhurst's funeral service was held in St John's, Smith Square (a church in which, incidentally, in early March 1914, there had been an explosion attributed to Suffragette activity.) Afterwards her coffin was taken to Brompton Cemetery for burial.

2 July 1928
After more than six decades of campaigning, the 'Representation of the People Act' was passed and all women finally got the vote in the UK on the same terms as men.

Millicent Fawcett was still alive and attended the Parliamentary session to see the vote take place. She wrote in her diary the same night, *"It is almost exactly 61 years ago since I heard John Stuart Mill introduce his suffrage amendment to the Reform Bill on 20 May 1867. So I have had extraordinary good luck in having seen the struggle from the beginning."*

PART TWO

SUFFRAGETTE STORIES

The Suffragette Timeline

SUFFRAGETTE STORIES

1. Adela Pankhurst
2. Suffragette postcards
3. Suffragette games
4. 'The Cat & Mouse Act'
5. Suffragists versus Suffragettes
6. Suffragette colours and medals
7. May Billinghurst
8. Frederick Pethick-Lawrence
9. The Suffragette Garden
10. Vera 'Jack' Holme
11. Nancy Astor MP
12. 'Black Friday'
13. Mary Jane Clarke
14. The Suffragette with the whip

1. ADELA PANKHURST

THE FORGOTTEN SISTER

When we think of the Pankhursts, the image that immediately springs to mind is one of Emmeline Pankhurst, the indomitable matriarch of the famous Manchester family. We are also accustomed to seeing pictures of the photogenic Christabel, her eldest daughter, and occasionally of Sylvia, the middle daughter, but sadly, the youngest daughter Adela has often been forgotten. Many thought she was too young to play a part in the Suffrage campaign, but quite the reverse was true. Adela Pankhurst, in fact worked tirelessly for the Women's Social and Political Union (WSPU) but for some reason, she never found favour with her mother.

Adela, born in June 1885, suffered from a range of childhood illnesses. She was born at a time when the Pankhursts were busy with her father Richard's political career and both Adela and her younger brother Henry were largely entrusted to a nurse for their upbringing. Adela struggled at times with her education and had to be withdrawn from Manchester High School for Girls after becoming depressed.

At the age of 16, Adela caught scarlet fever which left her with permanent lung damage. She was sent to Switzerland to recover and came back with a new passion, to become a teacher. Her mother was not pleased by this as it was seen the occupation of someone from a lower social class, but Adela was determined to follow through on her chosen path.

In 1903 when Emmeline and Christabel founded the WSPU in their front room in Manchester, Adela backed the family cause, and became one of their most confident speakers. She travelled the country, always available to speak when needed.

At one meeting in Manchester's Belle Vue Pleasure Park, she was arrested for smacking the hand of a policeman who told her she should be put to work as a washer woman! Seven days in prison meant the end of her teaching career.

For the next five years Adela worked tirelessly for the Union, travelling to remote parts of Scotland and never failing to put herself on the front line at rowdy meetings. In the summer of 1908, a huge women's suffrage rally was organised near Leeds and Adela spoke for over an hour to the 100,000 crowd. However, she was a slight, thin woman and often became ill through overwork. After an arrest at a rowdy meeting in Dundee, Adela and the other arrested Suffragettes went on hunger-strike, but she was deemed unfit for forced feeding; the doctor described her as a 'degenerate type'.

Although Adela carried on the Suffragette cause, usually away from her mother and sisters in London, she started to have misgivings about the more militant actions of the Union. And like her sister Sylvia, Adela became interested in socialism. Christabel even feared that she would try to start a new movement and, subsequently Adela was treated with suspicion and hostility.

In 1911, she left the Union for good and later said, *"The truth about my attitude, though I kept it to myself, was that I had come to realise that militancy was out of control… I knew all too well that after 1910 we were rapidly losing ground. I even tried to tell Christabel this was the case, but unfortunately she took it amiss."*
From this point, Adela felt abandoned by her family and had no money or job. She briefly worked as a gardener after her mother had offered to pay for the course on the understanding that she would never speak on a public platform in Britain again. However, gardening did not suit the rather frail Adela and eventually Emmeline bought her a one-way ticket to Australia, with an invitation to stay with her friend and suffrage campaigner Vida Goldstein. Adela would never see her mother or sisters again.

In Australia she was free from her family and became extremely popular. She was able to follow her socialist convictions, and in 1917, married Tom Walsh of the Federated Seamen's Union. They had a son and five daughters. She spoke openly against the war and, with her husband, joined the Communist Party of Australia. However, in the next few years, Adela drifted more and more towards the right and in 1929 founded the Australian Women's Guild of Empire, a reactionary body that condemned working mothers, contraception and trade unions. In her later years, she was known to despise communism and even defended fascism.

In 1928, just weeks before her death, Emmeline wrote to her daughter expressing regret at the wasted years. Years later, Adela gave credit to Millicent Fawcett and the Suffragists for winning the vote. As far as she was concerned, her mother and sister had given in to patriotism too easily at the start of the Great War. Adela later became one of the founding members of the right wing and nationalistic Australia First Movement. She visited Japan in 1939 and was arrested and interned in 1942 for her advocacy of peace with Japan.

Adela is undoubtedly the forgotten Suffragette as she was disowned by her own family, but she was a fiery and impassioned speaker whose talents were never properly recognised. She died in 1961.

2. SUFFRAGETTE POSTCARDS

One of the most notable things about the suffrage campaign was the strong passions that it aroused and the deep divisions it created in public opinion. This was reflected in the postcard art, often via extreme images, that was created for people to use in advancing their arguments.

Postcards had only been introduced into Britain in the late part of the 19th Century, but they did not become widely popular until 1902 when Britain became the first country to allow both address and message to be written on one side of the card, freeing up the whole of the other for the picture. As there were up to seven postal deliveries a day in large cities, it was possible to send someone a postcard in the morning inviting them to tea that afternoon!

Postcard manufacturers were quick to react and soon produced postcards not only with pictures of places, but also with images that reflected the politics and celebrities of the day. Suffragette postcards became hugely popular and allowed people to express their opinions on the subject by sending either a Pro or Anti-Suffragette postcard.

Anti-Suffragette Postcards

Most of the Anti-Suffragette postcards were very unflattering and now seem either deeply cruel or patronising. The Suffragettes were often portrayed as grumpy old women, extremely ugly with little round glasses and often with warts or hairs sprouting from their chin. Women were often characterised as spinsters, serving as a warning to women that if they supported the suffrage campaign, they might end up like this as well. The men who were shown with the Suffragettes were drawn as skinny, little men who looked worried and bullied, or were shown as being left at home to deal with crying babies, with no food on the table.

American anti-suffrage postcards often showed Suffragettes as little girls pretending to be grown-ups or as little kittens with collars and bows. Alternatively, men were portrayed as strong and dependable dogs, as bulldogs protecting Britain from all the 'votes for women' nonsense!

Many postcards that focused on some of the acts of militancy, showed the Suffragettes as unhinged and hysterical, smashing windows and setting fire to buildings in an irrational way.

Pro-Suffragette Imagery

The women's movement was determined to fight back with positive images. The Suffrage leaders recognised the importance of visual imagery and set about challenging some of the anti-suffrage stereotypes and replacing them with something better.
This was helped by the invention of the photograph postcard (c 1904-1905) which allowed the suffrage organisations to show the public what the leaders of the movement actually looked like. They could therefore portray the leaders as sensible, feminine women looking intelligent and rational. Christabel Pankhurst who was a Manchester University law graduate, was often shown in her graduation gowns. She became something of a pin-up for the Suffragettes as she was attractive, stylish and charismatic and her photograph was used on many postcards.

Postcards of marches and processions became very popular as they demonstrated the strength of support for their cause. Members of the public could see that the women in suffrage parades were not the man-hating ugly shrews depicted on the Anti-Suffragette postcards. They were disciplined and passionate, but also stylishly dressed and exuding femininity.

The Suffragette Timeline

They also helped to show the vast numbers of women involved in the processions. 13,000 women marched in the Procession of Women organised by the National Union of Women's Suffrage Societies (NUWSS) in June 1908 which was able to show, that counter to some politicians' claims, women's suffrage had mass support.

The Artists' Suffrage League (AFL), was established in 1907 to produce artwork for the "Mud March" in February of that year organised by the NUWSS. They were responsible for some of the most beautiful banners and posters used by the organisation in future marches. One of their most iconic images is the 'Bugler Girl', which was used to call women to demonstrations.

The Suffrage Atelier, was established in February 1909. This group of illustrators could produce work quickly in support of the Women's Social and Political Union (WSPU). Their most famous design and probably one of the most effective is the postcard called 'What a Woman may be, and yet not have the Vote' pictured here. Both these groups used their members' skills to great effect to galvanise sympathy and support for the cause.

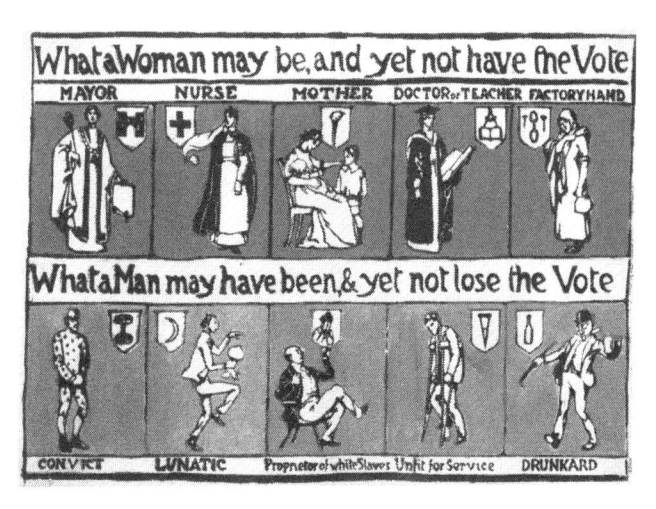

The Suffragette Timeline

3. SUFFRAGETTE GAMES

PANKO AND PANK-A-SQUITH

The Suffragette campaigners needed to fund-raise to support their organisations and so many shops sprang up around the UK, selling not only Suffragette newspapers and books but everything from hats to bicycles, often in the Suffragette colours of green, white and purple. Some of the most interesting items were the board and card games.

Panko, a card game, was sold by the Women's Social and Political Union (WSPU) as a marketing tool and to raise funds. It was marketed as a gift and advertised in 'Votes for Women' and other newspapers in December 1909 with the caption:-
"Not only is each picture itself an interesting memento, but the game produces intense excitement without the slightest taint of bitterness."

The Panko rules specified that all players should be split into Suffragists and the Anti-Suffragists and the game contained 48 cards which reflected some of the key moments and characters in the campaign.

101

The illustrations by political cartoonist, Edward T Reed, depicted Emmeline Pankhurst with her sash in colours of Purple, white and green, a Suffragette being escorted to the police station by a burly policeman and a group of Suffragettes trying to gain entry to the Houses of Parliament.

Christabel Pankhurst was shown with her arm raised in majestic fashion and upholding the law in her robes. Despite having a first-class law degree from Manchester University, as a woman she was not allowed to practice the law. The judge was depicted passing out a sentence of fourteen days while the other men in the court room sat laughing and sniggering. While, in the Holloway Jail, a rather posh looking Suffragette in a fur coat covered in the prison arrow symbol is seen refusing to eat at the 'Holloway Restaurant!'

Pank-a Squith was a board game which derived its title from combining the names of Emmeline Pankhurst, and that of the Liberal Prime Minister Herbert Asquith, and was first made available in 1908. In the game, a Suffragette attempts to move from her home to the House of Commons. To get there, she had to cross fifty squares, each with its own cartoon picture of the obstacles that were placed in the path of activists. Each square depicted scenes from the Suffrage campaign such as window smashing, marches and demonstrations. The players must try to avoid arrest, jail and forcible feeding on the way to their goal. The game came with 6 metal Suffragette pieces.

The Suffragette Timeline

4. THE 'CAT AND MOUSE ACT'

In 1913, the Suffragette struggle was at its height, many women who had been sent to prison for acts of protest, went on hunger-strike. The prison authorities, with the backing of the Liberal Government, started force feeding the Suffragettes via a tube forced into the nose or mouth and down the throat. This act of brutality resulted in many health problems for the brave women who endured it. Some Suffragettes were force fed hundreds of times.

The Government genuinely feared that one of the Suffragettes might die in prison from refusing to eat or being force fed and become a martyr for the cause. So great was their concern that they rushed through the 'Prisoners (Temporary Discharge for Ill-Health) Act', which became commonly known as the 'Cat and Mouse Act' which was passed on 25 April 1913.

This Act allowed the early release of prisoners, on license, who were so weakened by hunger-striking that their health was in danger. The released prisoners could have restrictions placed on their movements, and could be re-arrested for any subsequent misdemeanor and taken back to prison when their health recovered. Although forced feeding stopped, the authorities hoped the Act would enable them to control the militancy of the WSPU activists. The imagery of the 'Cat' (the Government) playing with the poor 'Mouse' before its ultimate demise, handed a propaganda victory to the Suffragettes, as the Liberal Government lost support for its decidedly illiberal treatment of protestors.

Ethel Smyth, (suffragette, composer and conductor) said about the Act in her memoirs:-

"The so-called 'Cat and Mouse Act', of which the murderous, cowardly, pseudo-humane refinement is to my mind more revolting than any torture invented in the Middle Ages, was now in full swing. The authorities dared not let the women die, so would release them, sometimes half-dead, to be rearrested as soon as they were judged fit to serve the remainder of their sentence. Whereupon the whole hideous business would begin again, the idea being that by degrees bodies and wills would be broken past mending. How a group of civilized Christian men could lend themselves to this proceeding rather than perform a simple act of justice already fifty years overdue is inconceivable - but so it was."

However, the Act proved somewhat ineffective as the authorities experienced much more difficulty than anticipated in re-arresting the released hunger-strikers. One of these escapees was Lilian Lenton, who had been arrested on charges of arson, including burning down the Tea Pavilion at Kew Gardens. While in Holloway she held a hunger-strike for two days before being forcibly fed, which caused her to become seriously ill with pleurisy caused by food entering her lungs. It took two doctors and seven wardens to restrain her. She was quickly and quietly released. Months later, on another arson charge, she had been released from Leeds Jail after starting another hunger strike and then managed to evade the police on several occasions. Even though the house she was living in was under surveillance, she disguised dressed herself as a young man and walked out under their noses! She then led the police a merry dance up and down the country escaping justice in Cardiff dressed as an old lady, managing to hobble to the station and onto a train for London. The inability of the Government to lay its hands on Lilian Lenton and other high-profile Suffragettes caused a public scandal, and gave a great propaganda tool to the cause.

The Suffragette Timeline

The Asquith government's implementation of the Act caused the militant WSPU and the Suffragettes to perceive Asquith as the enemy and partly led to an increase in support for the Labour Party.

5. SUFFRAGETTES VERSUS SUFFRAGISTS

During the most active years of the fight for women's suffrage (1908-1914), broadly speaking there were two distinct groups campaigning to obtain votes for women; the Suffragists led by Millicent Fawcett, and the Suffragettes led by Emmeline Pankhurst. There were many other smaller groups, like the Women's Freedom League who had split from the WSPU in 1908, but essentially divisions in the movement came from a profound disagreement about tactics.

The Suffragists believed in using constitutional methods such as letter writing, petitions and demonstrations. Millicent Fawcett had been married to the blind Liberal MP Henry Fawcett and she became his eyes and ears in Parliament. She was convinced that the route to women's freedom lay in convincing Parliament that women deserved the vote for their education, intelligence and hard work. Women should act with dignity and not do anything that would make them look irresponsible. She deplored the actions of the more militant Suffragettes – the window smashing, damage to letterboxes and arson.

As militancy increased the relationship between the two women and their organisations became increasingly strained and hostile. When Emily Wilding Davison died after running in front of the King's horse at the Epsom Derby in 1913, Fawcett did not attend the funeral or send a wreath or note of condolence.

However, relations between the two women had not always been as difficult. When Emmeline Pankhurst had first formed the Women's Social and Political Union in 1903, Millicent Fawcett welcomed their arrival as a way of injecting some fresh impetus into the movement. In the early days it was not uncommon for women to join both organisations and attend their different meetings and rallies.

In 1906, when the first Suffragettes started being arrested for doing little more than trying to see their MP's, Millicent Fawcett addressed a meeting of the NUWSS and said;

"Every kind of insult and abuse is hurled at women who have adopted these methods … But I hope the more old-fashioned suffragists will stand by them…… in my opinion, far from having injured the movement, they have done more during the last 12 months to bring it within the region of practical politics than we have been able to accomplish in the same number of years."

1906 was also the year that the word 'Suffragette' was first coined, originally by a hostile press as an insult, but the Suffragettes adopted it themselves as a way of showing that they were the group who believed in 'Deeds Not Words' and it became a useful way of differentiating between the two groups of women.

While relationships had been cordial, even friendly in 1906, over the next few years, the more militant actions of the Suffragettes drove a wedge between the two groups. In 1911, at the meeting at the Royal Albert Hall, Christabel Pankhurst said;

"We say to you non-militant women, do not sin against the light. Do not let cowardice blind your vision. Be honest with yourselves. Think this thing out clearly without any heat or emotion. Ask yourselves what is the good of a constitutional policy to those who have no constitutional weapon. We say for constitutional Suffragists, you are no longer children, and you must not play the part of children. You are women with the souls and minds of women, and you must quit yourselves like women. I will put two questions to you: Do you deny that these militant methods are necessary?...

The Suffragette Timeline

"*...History teaches you that they are; present day experience teaches you that they are. And again I ask you, 'Are Militant methods right?' Yes they are right. They are the only methods that are right. If we rely on constitutional methods when our intelligence tells us that these methods are in vain, then we are cowards. Morally and physically we are cowards. And that is not a thing that any woman likes to be.*"

This direct attack by Christabel on the law-abiding suffragists led to Millicent Fawcett withdrawing all support from the WSPU and writing letters to the press condemning their methods.

In 1912, when the arson campaign was started by WSPU supporters with the backing of Emmeline and Christabel Pankhurst, Millicent declared that the militants were, "*the chief obstacles in the way of success of the suffrage movement in the House of Commons.*"

The Suffragists had also decided to back the Labour Party and worked closely with other men's organisations, whereas Mrs Pankhurst did not really trust any politicians to deliver the vote.

When the First World War stated in August 1914, the two organisations again took different approaches. Emmeline and Christabel Pankhurst immediately suspended campaigning for the vote and threw themselves into the war effort. Millicent Fawcett and many members of the NUWSS, however, backed the peace campaign and continued campaigning for women's suffrage throughout the war.

6. SUFFRAGETTE COLOURS AND MEDALS

In the spring of 1908, the Women's Social and Political Union (WSPU) was planning a huge march and demonstration in London's Hyde Park to show the Government the true strength of women's feelings about gaining the vote. Emmeline Pethick-Lawrence, the Treasurer of the WSPU and the Editor of their newspaper 'Votes for Women', decided that the Union should have its own colours – purple, white and green. She said, *"Purple...stands for the royal blood that flows in the veins of every suffragette...white stands for purity in private and public life...green is the colour of hope and the emblem of spring"*.

Within a few weeks the colours had been adopted and were used on huge range of products from purses, buttons and pins to playing cards, jars of jam and even bicycles. At the march on 21 June 1908, thousands of women wore white dresses accessorised with purple and green which unified the procession and made it a brilliant sight. From that day onwards, in the minds of the British public, the Suffragettes would be forever known by the colours purple, white and green.

The Holloway Badge

The Holloway Badge or Brooch was designed by Emmeline Pankhurst's second daughter, Sylvia, and was presented with a special Illuminated manuscript also designed by her.

The badge, sometimes known as the 'Victoria Cross' of the WSPU, was cleverly designed to represent the portcullis symbol of the House of Commons, with the arrow worn by Suffragette prisoners superimposed on top in the Suffragette colours of purple, white and green It was introduced in April 1909 to be awarded to women who had been to prison for the cause and were first presented at a rally at the Royal Albert Hall in London.

Sylvia Pankhurst was a talented artist who had studied at Manchester Municipal School of Art and then won a scholarship to the Royal College of Art in London. She used her artistic talents to great effect for the WSPU and designed some of the most beautiful and iconic art from that period – the membership card for the Union, banners, posters and the iconic 'Angel of Freedom' used on a wide variety of items including Suffragette china.

The Hunger Strike Medal

This special medal was specifically designed for those members of the WSPU, who had gone on hunger strike while in prison. They were first presented in the Summer of 1909 after the first act of refusing food earlier that year by Marion Wallace Dunlop, the artist who had managed to apply the indelible ink stamp in the lobby of St Stephen's Hall earlier in the year.

The Medal consists of a ribbon in the Suffragette 'colours' of purple, white and green with a silver disc, engraved the name of the recipient.

Also, a silver pin bar engraved 'For Valour', a hanging length of ribbon, and either a silver or a striped enamel bar, from which hung a silver circle with the name of the hunger striker on one side and 'Hunger striker' on the other. If the Suffragette had endured forcible feeding, this could also be added to the inscription.

These medals were made by Toye, a well-known Clerkenwell firm still trading today, and cost the WSPU £1 each.

Many recipients proudly wore them, into old age, on suffrage occasions, and these medals are treasured today by collectors (and sell for thousands of pounds) who recognise the bravery of the women to whom they were awarded.

7. MAY BILLINGHURST

Have you ever wondered if you could have been brave enough to join the Suffragette cause, knowing that you might be open to brutality and imprisonment? Imagine the courage required to be disabled, in a wheelchair, and to still put yourself in such danger.

(Rosa) May Billinghurst was born in Lewisham in 1875 into a comfortable middle-class family but was left paralysed by illness when only five months old. Although she regained the use of her arms and hands, she would never walk unaided, and relied on a tricycle wheel chair.

In her twenties, she became involved in charity work in the Greenwich and Deptford Union Workhouse. She was shocked at the horrific conditions, but cared especially for the women who had been the victims of violent or drunk husbands, young girls who had been raped and made pregnant and women who had been left ill and destitute by the appalling working conditions in factories.

It was undoubtedly this work that turned the young May to politics and the Suffragettes. She said:

"It was gradually unfolded to me that the unequal laws which made women inferior to men were the main cause of these evils. I found that the man-made laws of marriage, parentage and divorce placed women in every way in a condition of slavery – and were as harmful to men by giving them power to be tyrants."

May Billinghurst joined the Women's Social and Political Union (WSPU) and became one of their most active members, founding the Greenwich branch. She took part in the 'Black Friday' demonstrations of 1910 and was one of the 159 women arrested. She was an impressive sight at demonstrations in her special tricycle decorated with the suffragette colours of green, white and purple.

After more arrests, she was sentenced to eight months in Holloway for damage to letterboxes and later recalled her brutal treatment while on hunger-strike:

"My head was forced back and a tube jammed down my nose. It was the most awful torture. I groaned with pain and I coughed and gulped the tube up and would not let it pass down my throat. Then they tried the other nostril and they found that was smaller still and slightly deformed, I suppose from constant hay-fever. The new doctor said it was impossible to get the tube down that one so they jammed it down again through the other and I wondered if the pain was as bad as chid-birth. I just had strength and will enough to vomit it up again and I see tears in the wardresses' eyes."

It took three doctors and five wardens to force feed May and her mouth was eventually forced open using iron pincers, losing a tooth in the process. The experience caused an outrage in the Press and led to questions in Parliament. She was released two weeks later on grounds of ill health. May went on to become a popular speaker, and 'marched' in the funeral procession of Emily Wilding Davison two months later. Undeterred by her suffering, in 1914, May took part in the deputation to petition the King which turned into a violent battle between Suffragettes and the police. At one point two policemen actually tipped May out of her tricycle but she was helped back in by other Suffragettes.

May carried on supporting the WSPU throughout the war and attended Emmeline Pankhurst's funeral in 1928. She spent the rest of her life quietly, first in a flat near Regent's park and then in Surrey where she passed away in 1953.

If you want to know more about May Billinghurst there is an excellent chapter in Fran Abram's book 'Freedom's Cause'.

8. FREDERICK PETHICK-LAWRENCE

THE SUFFRAGETTES' 'GREATEST MAN'

Frederick Pethick-Lawrence is one of the unsung heroes of the women's suffrage movement, and deserves to be better known for the important part he played. Fred and his wife Emmeline were dedicated and passionate supporters of votes for women, and one of the proudest moments of his life came when he was sent to prison for the cause.

Frederick Lawrence was born into a wealthy, Liberal family in West London and attended Eton followed by Trinity College Cambridge. He was a natural academic (studying Maths, followed by a second degree in Natural Sciences) but began to take an interest in social reform after visiting a 'university settlement' in Canning Town. It was here that he met the unconventional Emmeline Pethick. She smoked and was one of the first women to ride a bicycle. Emmeline was far more radical than Frederick and at first she refused to marry him because he remained neutral on the Boer War, while she was strongly against it. He was so keen to win her over, he even went to South Africa to see the situation for himself.

When they married in Canning Town, (with 50 guests from the St Marylebone Workhouse), they rejected convention by creating a double-barreled surname, rather than Emmeline taking her husband's name, and became the Pethick-Lawrences. They took a flat in Clement's Inn, Central London (which later played such a large part in the suffrage campaign) and a large house in the country for weekends.

In 1905, they read about the first act of Suffragette militancy by Christabel Pankhurst and Annie Kenney and wanted to know more. Labour MP Keir Hardie introduced them to Annie Kenney, and Emmeline started to become heavily involved in this new organisation

Frederick was reluctant at first, saying, *"I failed to see what the average sheltered woman of the middle classes had to complain about."* But when his wife was arrested and sent to prison, Fred decided that the WSPU needed his skills and in a short time, he hired more office space, and put the Union on a professional footing. They made an impressive team as Emmeline was a brilliant speaker and fund-raiser, whereas Fred was happy to work quietly in the background supporting his wife.

He also began to edit the 'Votes for Women' newspaper and provided financial support by bailing out the Suffragette prisoners from Cannon Row Station earning him the nickname of 'The Godfather'.

In 1912, the Suffragette movement started a new campaign of militancy instigated by Christabel Pankhurst. Fred, Emmeline and Emmeline Pankhurst were all arrested for conspiracy after the window-smashing raids of March 1912 (Christabel had escaped to Paris).

After their trial in May 1912, all three were sentenced to nine months in prison and Fred was sent to Brixton. Hearing that the women had gone on hunger strike, Fred followed suit and was force fed twice a day for ten days. By the time he was released he had lost one and a half stone but never complained about his ordeal.

After their release, the Pethick-Lawrences travelled to Boulogne to meet Christabel and her mother to discuss the issues facing the movement. Fred and Emmeline expressed their doubts about increasing militancy, especially the tactic of arson, fearing a backlash from both the public and their own supporters. Fred also thought that Christabel should return to the UK to face the courts, but she had other ideas.

The Suffragette Timeline

Shortly afterwards, they received a letter from Mrs Pankhurst stating that they should leave the organisation. They were shocked and hurt. Christabel (who they had thought of as a daughter and who had lived with them for five years) never spoke to them again. At a meeting at the Royal Albert Hall a few weeks later, Mrs Pankhurst stated that the Pethick-Lawrences had left the organisation after disagreements about militancy, and followers were left wondering if they were a 'Peth' or a 'Pank'.

Although the Pethick-Lawrences were allowed to retain control of 'Votes for Women', Christabel started a new newspaper that she edited called 'The Suffragette'. Fred stated afterwards that they decided to go quietly as they had no wish to damage to the organisation that they worked so hard to build.

They were also facing bankruptcy proceedings from the cost of the window smashing campaign. Bailiffs arrived at their home in Surrey and staged an auction of their belongings. Friends kindly purchased items to give back to them, but that didn't raise enough money and the costs were taken from Fred's estate. In fact, Fred's personal wealth may be one of the reasons why the Pankhurst's sought to expel the Pethick-Lawrences as they feared that the Government would try to go after Fred's money to seek compensation for the costs of militancy.

The Pethick-Lawrences did stay in touch with Sylvia Pankhurst who also shared their socialist views and had also been alienated by her mother and sister.

In 1914, Fred and Emmeline opposed the war: Emmeline helped to set up the Women's International League of Peace and Freedom (WILPF) and Fred became Treasurer of the pacifist Union of Democratic Control (UDC).

When he was conscripted in 1918, he became a conscientious objector, choosing to take a job as a farm labourer. He also stood for Parliament on a peace-ticket but was defeated.

After the War, Fred became involved in the Labour Party and in the 1923 General Election, won the seat of West Leicester, having the satisfaction of defeating Winston Churchill.

In the 1940's as Secretary of State for India in Clement Atlee's Government, he eased the way for Indian Independence striking up a great friendship with Gandhi. Clement Atlee said of Fred, *"It was given to few men to play a key role in two great campaigns of Liberation"*. In 1945 Frederick was elevated to the peerage as Baron Pethick-Lawrence of Peaslake.

In 1954, Emmeline, Lady Pethick-Lawrence, died after a series of heart attacks. Fred was bereft and gave up their Surrey house. In 1957 at the age of eighty-five, he married Helen Craggs, one of the many Suffragettes for whom he stood bail nearly forty years earlier, and they were married at Caxton Hall, scene of many a Suffragette meeting. Later that year, Fred and Helen visited India, as honoured guests by Gandhi.

Fred passed away in 1961 with Helen by his side. There is no doubt that the Suffragette movement owed a great deal to Fred (and Emmeline). He gave all his considerable abilities and skill to the movement and it may not have flourished without the firm financial footing created by his dedicated service.

9. THE SUFFRAGETTE GARDEN

There are many tales of quiet heroism within the suffrage movement, and story of the Blathwayt family from Somerset is undoubtedly one of these.

Linley Blathwayt, a retired British army Colonel, his wife Emily and daughter Mary held progressive political views and were all advocates of women's suffrage. After retiring, Linley purchased Eagle House with four acres of land just outside Batheaston in Somerset, which he turned into a Suffragette garden and a place of refuge for women involved in the movement.

In 1908, Mary Blathwayt, then twenty-nine years old, became involved in the women's suffrage campaign. She agreed to help the local branch of the WSPU and became great friends with many of the leading lights of the Suffragette movement, including Annie Kenney.

The Blathwayt's generosity to the cause became well known among the Suffragettes and the family built a summer-house in the grounds of the estate that was called the 'Suffragette Rest'. Members of the WSPU who had endured hunger strikes and forced feeding in prison were invited to stay at Eagle House to recuperate. Colonel Blathwayt decided to create an arboretum in a field adjacent to the house. Women were invited to plant a tree to commemorate their prison sentences and hunger strikes. On 23 April 1909 Emily Blathwayt recorded in her diary that Annie Kenney, Emmeline Pethick-Lawrence and Lady Constance Lytton all planted trees. Colonel Blathwayt, who was a keen photographer, took pictures of the women, which were often sold to raise money at WSPU events.

Mrs Pankhurst visited the house and gained back much of the weight lost during her hunger strikes, and two ponds in the garden became known as the 'Pankhurst Ponds'.

In addition to Emmeline, her daughters, Christabel and Adela also planted trees. After the visit of Christabel, Emily Blathwayt wrote in her diary: "Christabel has planted her cedar of Lebanon by the pond; it was raining all the time. There is a wonderful charm about Christabel; she looks sweet and not like her photo. She is quiet and retiring."

The summer of 1913 saw a further escalation of WSPU violence with the start of an arson campaign. In July attempts were made by Suffragettes to burn down several houses owned by MP's opposed to Votes for Women, including a house being built for David Lloyd George, the Chancellor of the Exchequer. This was followed by arson attacks on cricket pavilions, racecourse stands and golf clubhouses. In June 1913, a house was burned down close to Eagle House, and under pressure from her parents, Mary Blathwayt resigned from the WSPU.

However, Emily and Mary Blathwayt remained active in the less militant NUWSS. Mary Blathwayt continued to live in Batheaston until her death in 1962. However, sadly the land around Eagle House, was sold for a new housing development and the Suffragette garden and the arboretum were destroyed.

10. VERA 'JACK' HOLME

Vera 'Jack' Holme was one of those remarkable, larger-than-life women who populated the women's suffrage movement. She was born in Lancashire in 1881, with a talent for singing, acting and playing the violin. In 1908 she became a member of the D'Oyly Carte Opera company touring the country performing Gilbert and Sullivan light operas.

In that same year, she also joined the Actresses Franchise League (AFL) with other renowned performers including Ellen Terry, Lena Ashwell, Sybil Thorndike and Kitty Marion. The AFL was open to anyone involved in the theatrical profession and they sold suffrage literature and staged plays with a pro-suffrage message. At the same time Vera also became active in the Women's Social and Political Union (WSPU).

In 1909, the WSPU raised enough money to buy a car so Emmeline Pankhurst could travel to meetings in comfort. The new Austin car was painted and upholstered in the official colours of the WSPU, with a green body, a purple stripe and white wheels. Vera was known for her work in the WSPU headquarters and was asked to become the official chauffeur for the leaders. She undoubtedly enjoyed ruffling feathers when she would arrive at meetings and people were expecting a male chauffeur. She described how at one supporter's house the other chauffeur had been shocked and horrified to find that she was invited to dine with the other guests while the drivers were usually sent 'below stairs'.

Vera was a strong and determined woman who took great risks on behalf of the cause. It had become a tactic of the WSPU that wherever a Cabinet Minister was due to speak, a group of Suffragette supporters would be sent, ahead of the event, to raise sympathy for the cause.

For this reason, in 1909, Vera accompanied other Suffragettes to Bristol where Augustine Birrell (Secretary for Ireland) was due to speak. As no women were officially allowed into the meeting, Vera and a colleague managed to get into the Hall earlier in the day and climbed onto a narrow platform behind the organ pipes. When Birrell got up to speak they caused havoc by shouting out *"Votes for Women"*. The Stewards took quite a while to discover their hiding place and even longer to get them out.

Vera continued her work for the Suffragette cause and in 1911, set up home with her lover, Evelina Haverfield, another active Suffragette. Both Vera and Evelina supported Mrs Pankhurst's decision on the outbreak of The Great War to help Britain's war effort. In 1914, Evelina founded the Women's Emergency Corps, which helped organise women to become doctors, nurses and motorcycle messengers.

Vera was commissioned as a Major in the Women's Emergency Corps and in 1915 she was placed in charge of horses and trucks in the Scottish Women's Hospital Units sent to Serbia. After the war ended, Evelina returned to Serbia to work with orphaned children and it was here in 1920 that she died of pneumonia. In her will she left Vera Holme £50 a year for life and Vera became the administrator of the Haverfield Fund for Serbian children.

She spent the rest of her life in Scotland living with friends, where she passed away in 1969.

11. NANCY ASTOR MP

The first woman to take a seat as a Member of Parliament was not British and nor had she taken any part in the fight for women's suffrage.

Nancy Shaw, rather ironically, was a wealthy American divorcee who arrived in Britain with her sister in 1904 to make a fresh start after an unhappy marriage. Her complex personality, and tremendous wit, endeared her to English society, and in 1906, she married Waldorf Astor (a fellow American ex-pat, but one of society's most eligible bachelors), who was later elected as Conservative MP in Plymouth in December 1910.

They made their home at the rather splendid Cliveden Estate in Buckinghamshire, and Nancy became notorious for her sharp wit and humour which would stand her in good stead for the life of Britain's first woman MP. When her husband became Viscount Astor after the death of his father in 1918, he was elevated to the House of Lords and Nancy decided to stand for her husband's now vacant seat of Plymouth Sutton. She was elected in the by-election in 1919 and made history becoming the first woman to take a seat in the British Parliament.

However, that title of first woman M.P should have been taken by Constance Markievicz, who was elected to Westminster in the 1918 election. But as an Irish socialist and member of Sinn Féin, she chose not to take her seat in Parliament. The 1918 poll had been the first election in Britain in which some women (and all men) could vote and was also known as the Khaki Election as it came just after the end of the war.

Although Nancy had never been an outspoken advocate for women's rights she was a woman of deep convictions.

Despite being elected as a Conservative, in reality, she was more of an independent and campaigned on specific issues in her forthright manner. In her election manifesto, she pledged to campaign for 'Peace, Progress and Prosperity' and wanted to help women and children. Her election manifesto stated, 'Vote for Lady Astor and your babies will weigh more.'

She also once said, *"Women have got to make the world safe for men since men have made it so darned unsafe for women."*

Once in the House of Commons, she was true to her word and campaigned for women and children. She had an abhorrence of drink and blamed it for many of the problems in society including violence to women. In 1923 she was responsible for the first Private Members' Bill ever passed by a woman, the 'Intoxicating Liquor (Sale to persons under Eighteen) Bill'. She also campaigned on a variety of women's issues, including widows' pensions, employment rights, maternal mortality rates, nursery school provision and the raising of the age of consent.

Nancy Astor's strength was evidently needed as she was the only women in Parliament for two years, with many MPs even refusing to speak to her and making her life as difficult as possible. Winston Churchill later said, *"we hoped to freeze you out"*.

She was reported to have had the following exchange:
Astor: "If you were my husband, I'd poison your tea"
Churchill: "Madam, if you were my wife, I'd drink it!"

In the 1930s, Nancy and her husband spoke out against the rise of Nazism in Germany, but objected to the British preparations for war. The couple both backed Prime Minister Neville Chamberlain's policy of appeasement, which left her somewhat tainted and isolated amongst fellow MP's.

In later years, she was accused of certain anti-Semitic and anti-Catholic views, which lead to a gradual loss of popularity and isolation from mainstream thinking. In the 1930s, Nancy and her husband spoke out against the rise of Nazism in Germany, but objected to the British preparations for war. The couple both backed Prime Minister Neville Chamberlain's policy of appeasement, which left her somewhat tainted and isolated amongst fellow MP's. In later years, she was accused of certain anti-Semitic and anti-Catholic views, which lead to a gradual loss of popularity and isolation from mainstream thinking.

She represented her constituency in Parliament for twenty-six years and never lost an election, but in 1945, Nancy was persuaded to step down from politics by her husband and stated afterwards, *"I will miss the House: the House won't miss me."* She died in 1964, aged 84.

12. 'BLACK FRIDAY'

On 18th November 1910, one of the most violent confrontations of the Suffragette campaign took place. Due to the brutality of the police response to the demonstration, it became known as 'Black Friday'.

As the WSPU held its ninth Women's Parliament at Caxton Hall in Westminster, they learned that Prime Minister Asquith had decided that his Government would not give Parliamentary time to the latest 'Conciliation Bill', but instead that he would make a statement at a later date on the women's suffrage question. Immediately, a deputation was sent to the House of Commons, led by Mrs Pankhurst, Elizabeth Garret Anderson (Britain's first woman Doctor), distinguished mathematician and physicist Hertha Ayrton and Princess Sophia Duleep Singh.

The deputation of around three hundred women was met with ranks of police, and a running battle lasting six hours commenced, with over one hundred (men and women) arrested. Many of the reported assaults on the women were sexual in nature with many complaining afterwards of attacks on the breasts such as nipping, wringing, pinching and twisting designed to cause the most humiliation. In numerous acts of personal bravery, a number of women who had been attacked returned to Caxton Hall for rest and treatment, before heading back out to re-join the demonstration.

Emmeline Pankhurst said, *"We stood there for hours, gazing down on a scene which I never hope to look upon again."*

The Government began a cover-up of the violence that day. When The Daily Mirror published a photograph of Suffragette Ada Wright lying on the ground after a beating, the Government tried to prevent the paper from being distributed, and ordered that the negatives should be destroyed.

Winston Churchill, the Home Secretary, then refused to allow a government inquiry into the police brutality.

Overall, the day was a public relations disaster for the Government, with elements of the Press becoming increasingly sympathetic to the Suffragettes' cause. Left-wing journalist H.N. Brailsford and Dr. Jessie Murray (MD and feminist), published a report 'The Treatment of Women's deputations by the Metropolitan Police' in 1911, which collected evidence of the police brutality.

The violence on 'Black Friday' claimed the lives of two Suffragette protestors, as Mrs Pankhurst's sister Mary Clarke and Henrietta Williams each sustained life-threatening injuries, which led to their deaths a few weeks later.

The State's brutal response that day, led to a gradual change in tactics by the Suffragettes. With mass collective action causing such violence, the tactics began to shift towards attacks on property which could be carried out be demonstrators without such a risk of harm. Hence the campaign of window smashing, vandalising mail boxes, and ultimately arson attacks on Establishment targets became increasingly important to the struggle.

13. MARY JANE CLARKE

THE FIRST SUFFRAGETTE MARTYR

Emily Wilding Davison is perhaps the Suffragette whose amazing act of heroism in most widely known. On 4 June 1913, she was trampled by the King's horse at the Epsom Derby and died of her injuries four days later. Her funeral, attended by thousands was a major national event, and was exploited by Mrs Pankhurst's WSPU for maximum publicity.

However, Emily Wilding Davison was not the first Suffragette to die for the cause. That dubious honour belonged to Mary Jane Clark, who died on Christmas Day in 1910. She was Emmeline Pankhurst's younger sister. Born in Manchester, one of ten children, Mary was educated in Paris, along with her elder sister Emmeline. She was co-founder with Emmeline of the 'Emerson & Co.' shop in Hampstead Row. As a young woman, she worked decorating art-enameled fancy goods and was described in the 1891 census as a 'decorative artist.'

In December 1895, Mary married John Clarke. By 1904, she left him, and lived with her niece Sylvia Pankhurst. In the early years of the Women's Social and Political Union, Mary acted as Emmeline's deputy as Poor Law Registrar in Manchester. By February 1906, she was part of the inner-circle in the WSPU and in 1907 was appointed a full-time organiser.

In 1909, she led a group to Downing Street, was arrested and sentenced to one month in prison. After being released, she began speaking for the WSPU in Yorkshire and by the summer was the WSPU organiser on the south coast in Brighton. Her skill as a campaigner was recognised when she was put in charge of the WSPU's efforts in the General Election campaign in January 1910.

On 18 November 1910, she was arrested for window smashing, during the violent demonstrations known as 'Black Friday'. Held in Holloway Prison, she joined many other prisoners on hunger strike and was brutally force fed. Eventually released on 23 December, she sadly died two days later in a house in London. She was described in her obituary by Emmeline Pethick-Lawrence as, "the first woman martyr who has gone to death for this cause."

Mary Clarke was one of the best loved and fearless leaders of the WSPU and Suffragette colleagues described how she spoke every day on the Brighton sea front, come rain or shine. A wreath was laid on her coffin with the words, 'I am glad to pay the price of freedom,' the very words she had telegraphed to her Brighton comrades on her conviction in November.

The funeral passed off with little publicity, perhaps because the WSPU did not want to create a storm of publicity during the General Election campaign which was proceeding at the time. It is this comparison with the huge publicity that marked the funeral of Emily Wilding Davison, that has meant that the heroic sacrifice of Mary Jane Clarke is almost forgotten.

14. THE SUFFRAGETTE WITH THE WHIP

In December 1908, a young Suffragette named Helen Ogston achieved notoriety at a meeting in London's Royal Albert Hall when she decided to use a dog whip to defend herself at a political meeting. This event was to send shockwaves around Britain and the news even reached as far as America and Australia.

Helen came from a middle-class academic family in Scotland and graduated from the University of Aberdeen. She moved to London with her sister and took a job, and became an active member of Mrs Pankhurst's Women's Social and Political Union (WSPU), even speaking at their meeting in Hyde Park in the Summer of 1908
Helen was recruited to attend a meeting of the Women's Liberal Foundation at the Royal Albert Hall. The main speaker was Chancellor of the Exchequer, David Lloyd George, who had earlier promised that he would discuss the issue of 'Votes for Women'. However, the WSPU fearing that Lloyd George would be evasive on the issue, packed the meeting with their own supporters to call him out when the time came.

Helen had enough experience of Suffragette demonstrations to know it was becoming all too frequent that women would not only suffer extreme violence and manhandling, but also sexual assault. Fearing that the stewards at the event might be violent, and not wanting to take any chances, she told organiser Sylvia Pankhurst, that she intended to bring a dog whip to defend herself from indecent assault. Despite Sylvia asking her to consider using an umbrella instead, Helen still took the dog whip to the Hall.

When Lloyd George started to speak, women sprang up all over the Hall heckling the Cabinet Minister and demanding that he talk about 'Votes for Women'. As expected, Liberal Party stewards started to remove the women, and the violence used by them shocked the audience, most of whom had never seen anything like it.

The next day in The Times, the letters page was filled with expressions of horror that women could be treated in such a way in a 'civilised' country. Even the Manager of the Hall, Hilton Carter, wrote to The Times emphasising that the violence was not committed by any of the Hall's own stewards. The Manchester Guardian wrote that the ejections had been carried out 'with a brutality which was almost nauseating.'

Helen Ogston later wrote a letter to 'Votes For Women' giving her own side of the story and saying that she had been knocked over backwards, burnt with a cigar and struck in the chest. Despite offering to leave quietly the men had continued to assault her, so she had no choice but to use the dog whip to defend herself. However, the illustration that appeared in the London Illustrated News a few weeks later showed a tall deranged Amazonian woman trying to fight off several men.

Opinion was divided amongst Suffragette leaders about whether using the whip had been a wise course of action. Many believed that this sort of publicity had done the cause some harm, but Helen Ogston was recognised by others in the Union as a true heroine, especially in her own home town of Aberdeen. The incident was blamed for an upsurge in male violence against often peaceful women demonstrators, and weeks later in Maidenhead, Helen was chased off-stage at a Suffragette meeting by men dressed as women carrying whips.

However, one definite result from this meeting resulted in Lloyd George announcing that women would be excluded from all his future meetings, which perhaps showed his real interest in the suffrage cause.

SOURCES

Votes for Women – The Virago Book of Suffragettes, Edited by Joyce Marlow, Virago, 2012

The Suffragette Movement, Sylvia Pankhurst, Virago, 1978

Sylvia Pankhurst – The Rebellious Suffragette, Shirley Harrison, Golden Guides Press Ltd, 2012

Freedom's Cause – Lives of the Suffragettes, Fran Abrams, Profile Books Ltd, 2003

The Militant Suffragettes, Antonia Raeburn, Michael Joseph, 1973

Woman's Effort – A Chronicle of British Women's Fifty Years Struggle for Citizenship, 1865-1914, ?, Forgotten Books, 2015

The Women's Suffrage Movement, Molly Housego and Neil R Storey, Shire Library, 2013

My Own Story, Emmeline Pankhurst, Vintage Books, 2015

The Pankhursts – The History of One Radical Family, Martin Pugh, Vintage Books, 2008

The Ascent of Woman, Melanie Phillips, Abacus, 2003

East London Suffragettes, Sarah Jackson and Rosemary Taylor, The History Press, 2014

The Suffragette View, Antonia Raeburn, David & Charles, 1976

Vindication – A Postcard History of the Women's Movement, Ian McDonald, Bellew, 1989

The Suffragettes in Pictures, Diane Atkinson, The History Press, 1996

The Life and Death of Emily Wilding Davison, Ann Morley with Liz Stanley, The Women's Press, 1988

The March of the Women, Martin Pugh, Oxford University Press, 2000

Emmeline Pankhurst, A Biography, June Purvis, Routledge, 2002

Rebel Girls – Their Fight for the Vote, Jill Liddington, Virago, 2006

A Nest of Suffragettes in Somerset – Eagle House, Batheaston, B M Willmott Dobbie, 1979

Women's Suffrage – A Short History of a Great Movement, Millicent Fawcett, Amazon Reprint

The Women's Suffrage Movement in Britain and Ireland, Elizabeth Crawford, Routledge, 2006

The Women's Suffrage Movement: A Reference Guide 1866-1928, Elizabeth Crawford, UCL Press, 1999

Campaigning for the Vote – Kate Parry Frye's Suffrage Diary, Ed by Elizabeth Crawford, Francis Boutle, 2013

Suffragettes and the Post, Norman Watson, Robertson Printers, 2010

The Spectacle of Women – Imagery of the Suffrage Campaign, Lisa Tickner, Chatto & Windus, 1987

Votes for Women Newspaper, Google Newspapers, https://news.google.com/newspapers?nid=IMJZBBnUFLgC

For more about all things Suffragette, please visit my pages at:

**Facebook.com/SuffragetteLife
www.SuffragetteLife.co.uk**

Printed in Great Britain
by Amazon